American History

1000 Interesting Facts About the United States

Table of Contents

Introduction..1
Section 1: Exploring the Core Facts of American History....................................2
Native Americans and Life Before European Exploration....................................2
European Exploration and Colonization of the United States.............................6
The Great Awakening..9
The French and Indian War..12
The Boston Tea Party..15
The American Revolution...18
The Constitutional Convention and the Constitution of the United States.....22
The First President of the United States...25
The War of 1812..28
The Indian Removal Act and the Trail of Tears..31
The Civil War..34
The Old West...37
The Industrial Revolution...40
The Spanish-American War...43
World War One..46
The Women's Suffrage Movement...49
The Roaring Twenties...52
The Great Depression..55
World War Two..58
The Cold War and the Space Race...61
The Civil Rights Movement..65
The Gulf War and the War on Terror..69
The United States of America in the 21st Century..72
Section 2: Uncovering More Fascinating Facts of American History...............75
Major Political Events That Shaped Modern-day Politics...................................75
Sports Achievements during US History..79
Military Conflicts Fought by Americans..83
Technology Revolution in the US..87
The Women's Rights Movement in America...90
Music, Art, and Literature Movements during American History.....................93
Major Supreme Court Cases of the 20th Century...96
African American History and Culture in the US...101
Famous Explorers Who Founded Early Settlements in the US........................104
Economic Developments in the United States..107
Cultural Events That Influenced US History..109
Conclusion...113
Sources and Additional References..115

Introduction

Are you interested in uncovering the secrets of American history?

Do you want to explore the depths of America's past and learn about events, people, and technological advancements that shaped this great nation?

If so, **1000 Interesting Facts of American History** is your perfect guide. Our facts cover America's earliest history to recent events. Uncover fascinating facts related to major political events, sports achievements, military conflicts, technology, social movements, immigration, music, art, and literature.

Discover some of the major Supreme Court cases, African American culture and heritage, and presidential elections.

With **1000 Interesting Facts of American History** *at your fingertips, it's never been easier to learn all about America's rich past! Read on to start your journey!*

Section 1: Exploring the Core Facts of American History
Native Americans and Life Before European Exploration

This chapter will explore the fascinating history of *Native Americans and life before European exploration*. Let's take a look at thirty interesting facts about Native American cultures, beliefs, languages, tools, and art. We'll also discover how the indigenous people utilized nature to survive in harsh conditions and develop complex trade networks between different tribes across **North America.**

1. **Native Americans** have lived in **North America** for around twenty thousand years.

2. The term **"Native Americans" is broad.** There were likely over one thousand different tribes and cultures before European colonization. Each one had different beliefs and systems.

3. Many tribes had a concept called **"Sacred Hoop,"** where all living things were linked together and needed to be respected by each other. It represents the seasons, the universe, and **the life cycle. It has no beginning or end.**

4. Tribes used **sophisticated tools** made from stone, bone, shell, wood, and antlers, allowing them to hunt animals or fish more efficiently. They could also **build homes** faster.

5. Native Americans created **pottery out of clay.** The pottery was used for food storage or cooking purposes. They could last up to generations within some families.

6. The indigenous people **relied heavily on nature.** They grew plants such as corn and squash. They also hunted buffalo, deer, elk, and ducks.

7. **Native American cultures developed complex trade systems** between different groups across North America. They exchanged goods like copper jewelry or animal skins for things they needed from other tribes.

8. Native American tribes developed **their own languages.** The indigenous people in North America did not have writing systems, so they passed their histories down orally and through other means, such as wampum belts.

9. **Tribes believed** in many different spiritual beliefs, which were often based on nature or animals. These beliefs guided most of their daily life decisions.

10. Some tribes practiced **farming techniques** like terracing, which allowed them to grow food more efficiently with limited resources. This same technique is still used by farmers today!

11. Music was an integral part of native cultures. People would **sing, dance, drum, and play flutes** and other instruments. Music connected individuals in spiritual ceremonies and celebrations.

12. Some Native American religious practices included vision quests. A person would go off alone into nature to have visions or dreams **inspired by spirit guides**. These guides would provide guidance and direction on essential matters within one's life.

13. Native American cultures practiced various forms of art, including pottery, basket weaving, and painting on hides. **Art was usually meant to be spiritual,** although some things, like baskets, were used for practical purposes. Art could also be used to record stories and histories within the tribe.

14. **Tribes had their form of organized societies with leaders** who would oversee critical decision-making processes like how to distribute food. Each tribe was different, so not all tribes had the same kind of societal structure.

15. Most tribes believed that **land did not belong to an individual** but to all the people living on it. This concept was known as **communal property** and allowed different groups to share common resources.

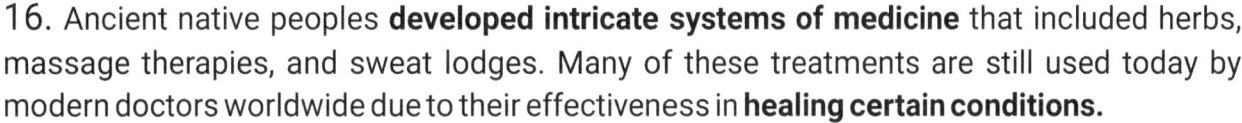

16. Ancient native peoples **developed intricate systems of medicine** that included herbs, massage therapies, and sweat lodges. Many of these treatments are still used today by modern doctors worldwide due to their effectiveness in **healing certain conditions.**

17. Native American **women were usually responsible for gathering food,** making clothing, and tending to the home. They also held various spiritual roles. They could be medicine women, healers, or leaders of ceremonies.

18. **Natives utilized astronomy** to predict seasonal changes and to understand the migration patterns of animals when certain plants would become ripe for harvesting. **This knowledge was essential for their survival.** They would plan activities around what nature provided them each year.

19. **Many tribes used deep-seated philosophies** that revolved around the balance between humans and nature, which they believed created harmony and happiness within one's life. This belief system has been passed down through generations of native peoples and is used even today!

20. **Native Americans** were known for their intricate beadwork designs, which could be found on moccasins, blankets, and other items. They **also made beautiful jewelry out of shells or stones** that had symbolic meanings attached to them. These pieces served a functional purpose and acted as powerful symbols. They represented something important about someone's identity within their tribe.

21. **Medicine men and women were significant within tribal societies.** These healers understood herbs and ritual and spiritual practices that could be used to treat illnesses or injuries. They passed this knowledge down to the next generation.

22. **Ancient tribes utilized the buffalo for more than just food**. They used the buffalo's hide for clothing, shelter, and tools like bows and arrows! Today, some native communities still practice traditional **buffalo hunting ceremonies** as part of their cultural identity.

23. **Native Americans followed migratory patterns** of animals throughout different seasons, allowing them access to fresh game on an ongoing basis. This was essential for their **survival during leaner months** when other resources might have been scarce due to a lack of rainfall or cold weather.

24. **Tribes relied heavily on the cycles of nature** when it came time to plant crops or harvest certain plants. They understood how their actions impacted the environment around them, so they took great care not to waste anything.

25. Three of the **most important crops in early North America were squash, maize (corn), and beans.** These three crops were called the Three Sisters. They were usually planted together. The cornstalk would act like a trellis for the beans. The squash's leaves would shade the ground, keeping the moisture in the soil so the **beans and maize could grow** without any problems.

26. **Fishing was an essential part of many native diets.** The indigenous people used unique methods like fish weirs (a trap made out of sticks), spears, and nets.

27. Ancient tribes developed ingenious ways of transportation. **They used canoes, which allowed them to travel across rivers easily.** They also used snowshoes which helped them traverse snowy paths and mountains.

28. **Some tribes built towns with palisades** (walls made out of wood) to protect themselves against potential threats. Palisades also provided protection during harsh winter months when **food might have been scarce** due to the lack of sunlight and cold temperatures.

29. **Native Americans believed in communicating respect between different cultures.** Traders exchanged not only goods but also stories, songs, and ideas, which allowed them to learn more about each other's customs and beliefs!

30. **Ritual dances** were often performed within native cultures as part of significant ceremonies or festivities. **These dances varied from tribe to tribe** but had some shared similarities, such as

European Exploration and Colonization of the United States

This chapter will explore the **history of European exploration and colonization** in the United States. We'll look at thirty interesting facts about how various countries claimed parts of North America, what they brought to the region, and why some colonies decided to declare independence. We'll also learn about other acquisitions, such as **Alaska, Hawaii, and Puerto Rico,** all of which eventually became part of the United States!

31. **The first European to explore North America was Leif Erikson.** He was a Viking. He traveled to what is now Newfoundland in 1000 CE.

32. By the time of **Christopher Columbus,** people had forgotten about Leif's voyage. Most early explorations were centered on Central and South America. The first European explorer to reach the present-day US was **Ponce de León.**

33. **Amerigo Vespucci**, who explored South America, is where we get the name "America."

34. **In 1607, England** established its first permanent settlement in North America at Jamestown.

35. **France settled colonies in Canada** and Louisiana in the 1600s.

36. **Spain** claimed much of the Southwest, from **California to Texas.**

37. **Dutch** colonists settled in New Netherland (present-day **New York**) in 1624.

38. **Pilgrims** came to Plymouth, **Massachusetts,** in 1620 on the Mayflower.

39. **Quakers** began settling in **Pennsylvania** in 1681.

40. **European settlers brought horses, cattle, pigs, and other animals to the Americas.** Settlers also introduced new plants like wheat, barley, oats, and rye for farming.

41. By the mid-1700s, **Britain's Thirteen Colonies** had been established along the Atlantic coast from Maine to Georgia.

42. **African slaves were brought to the United States** by European traders to work the plantations.

43. **The French and Indian War (1754–1763)** was fought between France and Britain with their respective Native American allies.

44. **Britain won the war** and gained control of much of eastern North America.

45. After the war, the **British attempted to increase taxes** on the colonists to pay off the war. The colonists were upset because they were not given representation in Parliament.

46. **The American Revolution** broke out in 1775 because of tensions between the Thirteen Colonies and Britain.

47. **The Thirteen Colonies declared independence** from Britain in July 1776.

48. **The Revolutionary War officially ended in 1783** with the Treaty of Paris. The treaty formally recognized the United States as an independent nation.

49. **Great Britain ceded most of its land** east of the Mississippi River to the United States.

50. **The Northwest Ordinance was passed in 1787.** It organized the area northwest of the Ohio River into the Northwest Territory, which would later become several states.

51. **The Louisiana Purchase of 1803** doubled the size of the United States.

52. **The Lewis and Clark Expedition**, which lasted from 1804 to 1806, was led by Meriwether Lewis and William Clark. With the help of a young Shoshone woman named Sacagawea, the party traversed the country from the Missouri River to the Pacific Ocean. They encountered Native American tribes and brought back valuable information, which expanded the knowledge of the American West.

53. **Florida became part of the United States** after the Adams-Onís Treaty with Spain in 1819.

54. After **the Mexican-American War**, Mexico ceded present-day California to the United States through the Treaty of Guadalupe Hidalgo in 1848.

55. **The Gadsden Purchase added land in southern Arizona** and southwestern New Mexico in 1853.

56. **Alaska was purchased from Russia** in 1867.

57. The United States acquired Hawaii and Guam in 1898. **Hawaii became a state in** 1959. Guam is a US territory today.

58. **Puerto Rico became a US territory** in 1898 following the Spanish-American War.

59. The **Panama Canal Zone** was leased to the US in 1903.

60. The **US acquired the Virgin Islands from Denmark** in 1917.

The Great Awakening

You might be wondering how we got through America's history so quickly. Don't worry! We will take a closer look at the big events of US history. This chapter will explore the **Great Awakening, a religious movement that swept across America** in the early to the mid-18th century. We'll take a look at how this spiritual revival challenged traditional Puritan beliefs and brought new **denominations of Christianity into the colonies,** such as Methodism. Additionally, we'll learn about why **George Whitefield** was so important to this period and discover why the Second Great Awakening sparked social movements, including abolitionism, temperance, and women's rights. These movements helped shape much of what **defines the people's sense of morality in the US today.**

61. **The Great Awakening was a religious movement** in the early to the mid-18th century.

62. It began with an emotional sermon by preacher **Jonathan Edwards in 1734**. The ideas from his sermon quickly spread, leading to a large turnout at revival meetings throughout America.

63. His sermon talked about how people were natural-**born sinners and how they needed to be forgiven** to attain salvation. He urged people to accept God into their lives.

64. **This spiritual awakening challenged traditional Puritan beliefs.** Puritans believed that only priests could interpret the Bible.

65. In the past, **free-thinking Puritans, like Anne Hutchinson,** had been banished from Puritan society for going against the norm.

66. **George Whitefield** was one of the leading preachers of the Great Awakening. He traveled up and down the East Coast, preaching his message of religious revival to thousands at a time.

67. **Whitefield's stirring sermons** promoted self-determination for individuals instead of depending on group consensus. His ideas inspired people to become more independent thinkers, not just believers or followers.

68. For example, he encouraged colonists to take control of their own lives by making decisions about **what kind of values they wanted.**

69. **The Great Awakening significantly impacted American intellectual life,** inspiring people to create their own interpretations of the Bible and helping them move away from traditional Puritan beliefs.

70. It also helped spark a **sense of national unity,** as colonists from different backgrounds united in their belief in God's power.

71. **The Great Awakening was an essential factor in the American Revolution.** It helped spread ideas about self-determination and liberty throughout the colonies before hostilities began with Britain.

72. **It encouraged people to think for themselves,** question authority, and stand up against oppressive forces, ultimately leading them toward independence from a monarchical system.

73. **New Protestant denominations** arrived in America because of the Great Awakening, such as Methodism.

74. **John Wesley founded Methodism** in the 1730s. In 1784, Methodism took root in America, with immigrants from Ireland bringing the religion with them.

75. **Baptists were also affected by the Great Awakening.** Baptists had been around since the 17th century, but the religious revival brought about a new kind of Baptist, one that broke away from Puritan (or Congregationalist) views.

76. There had been few Baptists in America before the Great Awakening. By 1804, there were over **three hundred Baptist churches in New England** alone.

77. Many prominent figures, including **Thomas Paine**, wrote extensively about religious liberty, **the separation between church and state**, and other topics related to individual rights and freedom of expression.

78. **The Great Awakening was a reaction to the Enlightenment,** which began in Europe. The Enlightenment was based on reason, while the Great Awakening was based more on emotion and beliefs.

79. **The Enlightenment affected religion.** Since the ideas of the movement were based on reason, there was increasing skepticism toward traditional Christian beliefs. Some **intellectuals rejected biblical theology** altogether, influencing what is now known as secular humanism today. Most Enlightenment thinkers called for religious tolerance.

80. **Deism emerged during the Enlightenment.** It rationalized the existence of God. Deists believed in God but did not believe he interfered in daily life. Some famous Deists were **Thomas Jefferson and Thomas Paine.**

81. Although the religious revival movement did not focus on rationalism, it still left a lasting impact on education in America. **Several famous universities opened because of the Great Awakening,** such as Princeton, Dartmouth, and Brown.

82. These universities were originally intended to be places **where men could learn about the Bible** and train to become ministers.

83. This movement was significant for **African Americans**. They were encouraged by preachers like Whitefield to **reject slavery and pursue freedom through faith** in Christ's teachings about love and justice for all people, regardless of race or class status.

84. **The Second Great Awakening** happened during the early 19th century. It is generally believed to have lasted from 1790 to 1840. It was another major Protestant revival.

85. The Second Great Awakening spurred several social reform movements, including **abolitionism, temperance, and women's rights.**

86. The Second Great Awakening preached that **all men were equal under the eyes of God,** leading to increased calls for abolitionism.

87. It also revived **the belief that one should live a life free of sin.** Temperance movements took this idea and applied it to the vice of drinking in excess.

88. The increased religious enthusiasm of the period empowered **women to take on a more active role in religious life, including teaching and preaching**. While women were still largely excluded from formal positions in religious institutions, the Second Great Awakening allowed them to gain greater autonomy and influence in religious matters.

89. The Second Great Awakening also contributed to a **growing sense of religious equality between men and women,** paving the way for the early women's rights movement.

90. **The Third Great Awakening took place from the late 1850s to the early 20th century**. This revival also focused on social issues like abolitionism. It also focused on the end times and the Second Coming of Christ.

The French and Indian War

This chapter will explore the **French and Indian War,** which was a theater of the Seven Years' War.

We'll take a look at **thirty interesting facts** about how this conflict began, who was involved in it, and what the outcome was. Learn about famous figures like **George Washington** and **Benjamin Franklin,** who played important roles during this war.

91. **The French and Indian War** was fought between 1754 and 1763 in North America.

92. This war was a theater of **the Seven Years' War,** which broke out over territorial disputes.

93. **The French and Indian War pitted the British** against the French. Both sides had Native American allies.

94. The war started because of disputes over land ownership of **the Ohio River Valley.**

95. **France helped its Native American** allies by providing weapons to prevent British colonists from expanding into new lands.

96. **The first battle** during this war took place at **Jumonville Glen** near present-day Pittsburgh, Pennsylvania, **in May 1754.** It only lasted about fifteen minutes.

97. **George Washington** commanded the colonists in the Battle of Jumonville Glen.

98. **Jumonville was the leader of the French forces** in the battle. He was sent to warn Washington to leave the area, not to engage in combat. **Jumonville died in the battle.**

99. **The first political cartoon in US history** was printed in 1754. The cartoon was designed **by Benjamin Franklin.** It showed the colonies as parts of a chopped-up snake.

100. **The Battle of Fort Necessity** was the first major battle of the war. It took place in July 1754. **George Washington** was forced to surrender the fort.

101. **British General Edward Braddock** was killed while leading a force against Fort Duquesne (now located within modern-day Pittsburgh) on July 9th, 1755, making him one of many casualties during this long and bloody conflict.

102. Initially, the **French** did better in the war. But the tides began to turn when the **British scored a victory** at Fort Niagara in July 1759. Their win allowed them to begin plans to invade Canada from the west.

103. **The Battle of Quebec** took place in September 1759. **The British had laid siege** to the city for three months before they were finally able to declare victory. Generals from both sides were killed from injuries they received while fighting.

104. **The French tried to retake Quebec**, but they failed.

105. Due to a lack of resources, both sides resorted to using **guerilla warfare tactics**.

106. **Over forty thousand colonists and British soldiers took part in the war.** The French had around ten thousand regulars. However, the French had more Native American allies than the British.

107. In September 1760, **the British successfully took Montreal.** The seizure of Montreal meant that all of New France was in British hands.

108. **In 1763, a peace treaty was signed in Paris between France, Britain, and the other countries that fought in the Seven Years' War.** The treaty ended that war and the French and Indian War. It gave all lands east of the Mississippi River to Britain. France withdrew from North America, although it kept some territories in Canada.

109. **Louisiana was split in half,** with Britain getting the eastern side. France got the western side.

110. **France would not hold Louisiana for long.** Before the 1763 Treaty of Paris, France signed a secret agreement with Spain. **France agreed to give Louisiana to Spain.** Shortly after the war, Spain received its half of the territory. It did not contest the terms of the Treaty of Paris.

111. The British were worried about its new residents in Canada, namely Catholics in Acadia. **In 1755, the British began expelling the Acadians.** Hundreds of them settled in Louisiana. The name "Acadian" turned into "Cajun." Cajuns still live in Louisiana to this day.

112. **The Treaty of Paris also gave all of Spanish Florida to Britain.** Spain had fought with France in the Seven Years' War and was forced to give up territories in the treaty.

113. Although this conflict was fought **primarily between Great Britain and France,** Native American tribes were significant participants. Most tribes supported France. Some even tried to remain neutral during the war.

114. **The Iroquois Confederacy was initially neutral in the war.** The Iroquois later allied with the British. However, members joined forces with the French. It really depended upon who offered better terms at any given moment.

115. **The French and Indian War** opened up opportunities for colonists from Europe to begin settling newly acquired territories. To do so, they had to push the indigenous people out.

116. **Native Americans** were not included in the peace treaty between France and Britain. They continued facing displacement from their lands until treaties were made directly with tribes or governments set up specifically for them.

117. **When France left, the Native Americans** lost an important trading partner. Although the colonists still traded with the natives, they didn't trade as many weapons and gunpowder.

118. **It is hard to know exactly how many people died in the war.** Historians estimate that eleven thousand died. Most of the people died from diseases.

119. British officers like **George Washington** gained experience and respect in the French and Indian War. His accomplishments in this war later led him to be commander of the Continental Army.

120. Other prominent figures in US history, such as **Benjamin Franklin**, played significant roles in the war as well. **Franklin became a commander in the war.**

The Boston Tea Party

This chapter will cover the events and causes of **the Boston Tea Party,** which was a **pivotal moment in United States history.**

The American Revolution would break out less than two years later. We'll look at **thirty interesting facts** about this historical event, from who organized it to what happened afterward. Learn why **Americans boycotted tea from England.**

Discover how the Boston Tea Party sparked future protests. We'll also explore other details, like what disguises were worn by the protestors!

121. **The Boston Tea Party was a political protest** that happened on December 16th, 1773, in the city of Boston, Massachusetts.

122. **Three ships carrying tea from England were sent to the harbor in Boston.** Colonists were upset about the fact they did not have representation in the British Parliament. To show their displeasure, they threw all 342 chests of tea into the water!

123. **The tea that was dumped** would have been worth almost two million dollars today!

124. The tea would have weighed over **ninety thousand pounds**.

125. In May 1773, **Britain passed the Tea Act.** This was one of many acts that upset the American colonists.

126. **Colonists already paid taxes on tea** because of the Townshend Acts, which were passed in the late 1760s. Colonists also paid taxes on glassware, stamps, and paper, to name a few.

127. During that period, **tea was very popular in America**. The colonists drank over one million pounds of tea a year in the late 18th century!

128. **The Tea Act gave the East India Company a monopoly on tea.** Smuggling was a big problem in the colonies. Almost 90 percent of the tea the colonists drank had been smuggled. It became clear to the colonists that the tax on tea would stand.

129. **Thomas Hutchinson was governor of Massachusetts** at the time of the Boston Tea Party. He wanted the taxes paid on the tea. He refused to let the ships leave the harbor with the tea.

130. **The colonists made it clear they would not pass the tax.** The captains didn't want to risk any potential damage to their ships, so they stayed in the harbor.

131. Over **one hundred people participated** in the historic **Boston Tea Party**. Only about sixty of them boarded the ships.

132. Most participants wore disguises, such as masks. Some even **dressed up as Mohawks**!

133. Participants used hatchets and ropes to dump the chests into the water. **It took them almost three hours in the dark to unload all the tea!**

134. The main organizer of this event was **Samuel Adams.** He is considered one of the Founding Fathers. He was also an active member of a political **group called the Sons of Liberty.**

135. **The Sons of Liberty** fought for the colonists' rights. This group could sometimes be violent. For instance, **they tarred and feathered officials**. A person would be stripped naked. Tar would be poured on them. And then feathers would be thrown at them.

136. Some of the famous Sons of Liberty include **Samuel Adams, Benjamin Church, John Hancock, Paul Revere, and Benedict Arnold.**

137. The Boston Tea Party was called the **"Destruction of the Tea"** at the time. Other cities had their own "tea parties," but the one in Boston was the most destructive.

138. Even though no fatalities or injuries were reported during this event, **the British were still furious**. They demanded compensation for the loss of the tea.

139. Britain passed several acts known as the Intolerable Acts. These acts restricted colonial rights even more, leading to more protests.

140. The Boston Port Act was passed first. The colonists had to repay the cost of the destroyed tea. Until they did, the port of Boston would be closed.

141. The Massachusetts Government Act put Massachusetts under the control of the British government. Prior to this act, Massachusetts had a charter. People in Massachusetts could also only have one town meeting a year.

142. The Administration of Justice Act allowed **British officials to be tried in Britain**, not in Massachusetts.

143. People were upset about this act because British soldiers had been given a fair hearing after **the Boston Massacre.**

144. In the Boston Massacre, **British soldiers fired into a large crowd of colonists.** The colonists had been pelting the soldiers with rocks and other objects. The captain never gave orders to shoot. Most of the soldiers were acquitted.

145. **The Quartering Act** required that housing be provided to British troops. This act applied to all Thirteen Colonies.

146. This historic act of rebellion **caused a lot of tension between Britain and America**. The Intolerable Acts did not ease the tensions. A revolution would eventually break out in April 1775.

147. **The Intolerable Acts** were meant to break the colonists' spirit. Instead, it **drew the colonists closer together.** In September 1774, twelve colonies sent representatives to the First Continental Congress.

148. **After the Boston Tea Party,** many Americans began drinking coffee instead of tea. Coffee was already popular in America, but coffee drinkers eventually outpaced tea drinkers!

149. Today, you can visit **several museums** dedicated to teaching visitors about the history behind what happened at **the Boston Tea Party**. You can even take boat tours where they dumped those 342 chests into the harbor waters!

150. To commemorate the anniversary of the Boston Tea Party, **a reenactment is held in Boston**. Participants wear traditional colonial clothing and even throw tea into harbor waters just like they did back then!

The American Revolution

This chapter will examine the **American Revolution and its lasting effects on the United States.** We'll explore how it began, who was involved, and what events led up to it.

Learn some **facts about the key battles** fought during this war, like Bunker Hill and Yorktown. Discover France's involvement, the treaty signed in Paris after the **colonists won their freedom from Great Britain,** and the contributions made **by African Americans and women.**

151. **The American Revolution began in 1775** and officially **ended in 1783.**

152. It was primarily fought between **the British and the colonists** of what would become America. Both sides had help from allies. The US had help from France, Spain, the Netherlands, and the Native Americans. The British had help from the Native Americans. They also received help from the Hessians.

153. **The leading cause of the conflict was taxation without representation.** Many acts had been passed that placed taxes on everyday goods. However, the colonists had no voice in Parliament. As the years passed, it became clear to them that their opinion had little weight in Britain.

154. One major event that propelled the colonists to fight a revolution was t**he Boston Massacre.** On March 5th, 1770, **British troops fired upon a crowd of angry colonists**. Five colonists were killed, creating more anti-British sentiment.

155. Another major event happened on December 16th, 1773. A group of colonists disguised as Mohawks threw hundreds of crates of tea into Boston Harbor to protest the Tea Act. This event is known as **the Boston Tea Party**.

156. **The First Continental Congress** was formed on September 5th, 1774. The representatives talked about effective ways to deal with the British government. **They sent a petition to the king,** asking him to remove the Intolerable Acts. The men agreed to meet again if things did not change. The First Continental Congress disbanded almost two months after it had started.

157. **John Adams wrote the Novanglus** essays, which were first published in 1774. These essays defend the constitutionality of the Stamp Act but argue the colonies had a right to **self-government.** His writing showcased his intellectual prowess, earning him the respect of his peers. John Adams was a noted figure in colonial America and would later become president.

158. On March 23rd, 1775, **Patrick Henry** gave his famous **"Give me liberty or give me death"** speech at St John's Church in Richmond, Virginia, while urging Virginia to raise troops for the American Revolution. He wanted people to realize that war was inevitable.

159. In 1775, **Thomas Paine** began writing his famous pamphlet called **Common Sense.** This work argued for American independence from Britain. It was not published until January 1776. Common Sense became one of the most widely read documents. By the end of the war, it is estimated that 500,000 copies had been sold!

160. **Paul Revere made his famous ride from Boston to Lexington** to warn Americans about British troops on April 18th, 1775.

161. **The British were planning** to take weapons and other supplies because they feared the colonists were on the verge of rebelling violently. Their actions **started the American Revolution.**

162. The **"shot heard 'round the world"** happened at the Battles of Lexington and Concord. The battle at Lexington was minor. At Concord, the two sides were at a standoff until someone fired a shot. To this day, no one knows which side fired first.

163. Shortly after the Battles of Lexington and Concord, **the Second Continental Congress was convened**. It essentially acted as the government while the colonies fought for their independence.

164. **George Washington was appointed commander** in chief of the Continental Army on June 15th, 1755.

165. **The Battle of Bunker Hill** was fought on June 17th, 1775, and is one of the most famous battles of the American Revolution. Although the British won, they suffered heavy casualties. The British soon realized this **rebellion would not be put down easily.**

166. **The Declaration of Independence** was adopted on July 4th, 1776, with Thomas Jefferson being its principal author. John Adams, Benjamin Franklin, Robert Livingston, and Roger Sherman edited or wrote portions of it.

167. **Thomas Jefferson** also wrote the Virginia Statute for Religious Freedom in 1776. The statute proclaimed that no one should be persecuted based on religion, despite their beliefs or lack thereof. This document was a precursor to the **First Amendment of the United States Constitution**.

168. The Battle of Trenton was fought on December 26th, 1776, when **George Washington's** forces crossed the Delaware River. **The colonists surprised the Hessian soldiers** stationed in the city. It was one of the most significant victories for the Americans during its war of independence. Winning the battle boosted morale greatly, which was suffering after defeats in New York.

169. On July 31st, 1777, **a French aristocrat named Lafayette became a major general** in the Continental Army. Lafayette played a major role in securing help from France.

170. Although the **French didn't really get involved in the war until 1778**, France played an essential role in helping the Americans win their freedom. For instance, French fleets helped blockade seaports so that British soldiers could not sail to America. In 1780, **French general Rochambeau's army arrived** to help the colonists. His assistance in the Battle of Yorktown was invaluable.

171. **Native Americans** were caught in the middle of the war, with many tribes fighting for both sides. For instance, **the Cherokee and Choctaw sided with Britain**. The Iroquois Confederacy was divided, although most tribes supported the British.

172. **Women also played an active role in the American Revolution** by serving their country. They nursed wounded soldiers, acted as spies, and even took up arms against the enemy!

173. **Betsy Ross is credited with creating the first United States flag** with stars and stripes representing the Thirteen Colonies. However, there is no firm evidence that she was the first to make the design. This **flag was adopted on June 14th, 1777**.

174. During the American Revolution, **African Americans played a crucial role in the war** effort. About 100,000 enslaved African Americans escaped. **Many joined the British forces,** hoping to find freedom. Other African Americans served as spies, messengers, and scouts. African Americans also served as soldiers in the **Continental Army.**

175. In 1777, **the Articles of Confederation** were created by the Continental Congress. The articles established the **first form of government for the United States**. A little over ten years later, the Articles of Confederation were replaced with the US Constitution after realizing too much power rested with individual states. The Constitution created the foundation of the **federal system of the US today!**

176. **The Battles of Saratoga** were fought between British and American forces in September and October of 1777. These conflicts turned the tide of the war in favor of the Americans and led them **to gain support from France.**

177. **The siege of Yorktown** lasted from September 28th to October 19th, 1781. American and French troops laid siege to the town for three weeks. **British General Cornwallis** was eventually forced to surrender. The end of the siege ended the major military operations of the American Revolution.

178. **The Treaty of Paris** was signed on September 3rd, 1783. It officially recognized **the United States as an independent nation.** The new nation gained everything north of Florida, south of Canada, and east of the Mississippi River.

179. **Benjamin Franklin**, **John Adams,** and **John Jay** helped negotiate **the Treaty of Paris.** France, Spain, and the Netherlands signed separate treaties with Britain.

180. **After winning freedom from Great Britain,** America began establishing its government and drafting laws and regulations, leading to what we know today as the present-day US.

The Constitutional Convention and the Constitution of the United States

This chapter will explore the history and key elements of **the Constitutional Convention** and **the Constitution of the United States.**

With these **thirty facts**, you'll gain insight into how **the Founding Fathers** created a document to ensure citizens had rights, freedom from oppression, and unfair treatment by others and the government. We will also examine the **Bill of Rights**, which outlines important freedoms.

Finally, we'll learn why understanding this **revolutionary document** is so critical to keeping America strong.

181. **The Constitutional Convention** was a meeting of delegates from the former Thirteen Colonies **in 1787** to discuss and form a plan for how the new nation would be governed.

182. **Rhode Island did not attend** the Constitutional Convention. It was worried that the new document would take away the state's power. Rhode Island was the last state to ratify the Constitution.

183. Many of the men who met at the Constitutional Convention became known as the **Founding Fathers.** These men helped establish the new nation. Some scholars believe all the men at the Constitutional Convention were Founding Fathers because they helped work on the US Constitution.

184. Some important **Founding Fathers** did not sign the Constitution. **Thomas Jefferson and John Adams** were away in Europe during the Constitutional Convention, so they did not get to sign the document.

185. The men who met at the convention wanted to ensure **citizens had rights**, including freedom from oppression and unfair treatment by others or governments. It was important to them that the new nation did **not become like Britain**.

186. At first, there were arguments about **how much power each state should have** and what kind of laws should apply across America.

187. But eventually, they agreed on a system. **Congress would have specific powers,** while individual states would have some control over their affairs. This is known as **federalism.**

188. It took the men at **the Constitutional Convention** four months (from May to September) to write their ideas down into one document. This document became **the Constitution of the United States.**

189. **Jacob Shallus**, a clerk from Pennsylvania, transcribed the document. He was paid $30, which would be around $730 today.

190. It took **ten months for enough states** to ratify the Constitution so it could become law. Some people were worried that the Constitution gave too much power to the central government.

191. Although seventy delegates were appointed to **the Constitutional Convention**, only fifty-five showed up. And of those fifty-five, only thirty-nine signed. Some became sick, and others left. But some outright refused to sign the document because of the lack of a **Bill of Rights**.

192. **The Constitution** set up three branches of government: **executive** (the president and his staff), **legislative** (Congress), and **judicial** (the Supreme Court).

193. This system ensures that no branch can become too powerful over the other. It's called **the separation of powers** or the system of checks and balances.

194. **The Constitution** also allowed for amendments, which are changes to the Constitution to suit the nation as time goes on.

195. The original **Constitution** did not mention **women** or **enslaved** African Americans.

196. **The Bill of Rights** was written four years later to ensure that everyone had access to basic rights. These rights include the **freedom** of

speech, religion, protest,** and more. However, some groups of people, like women, African Americans, and Native Americans, didn't get to enjoy these rights until later on. **The Bill of Rights is the first ten amendments to the Constitution.**

197. **The Constitution** replaced **the Articles of Confederation**. The Articles of Confederation gave more power to the states, and the US needed a stronger central government after the war.

198. The Constitution also set up **the Electoral College.** Today, people in the US cast their votes for president. Each state gets a certain number of electoral votes, depending on its presence in Congress. The new president is determined by how many electoral votes they receive. So, it is possible for a president to lose the popular vote (the vote of the people) while still winning the electoral vote.

199. **The Constitution** also outlines the process for electing senators and representatives to Congress. These people act as a state's voice in government.

200. However, **the original Constitution did not state that everyone had the right to vote**. The decision on who could vote belonged to the states.

201. This document helps to **protect us from the abuse of power by federal, state, and local governments** so that no one person could ever rule over the people without their consent.

202. **The Constitution states** that both houses of Congress must approve laws before they can become official laws.

203. **It forbids states** from making certain agreements with each other or foreign countries without permission from Congress first.

204. **The Constitution** can only be changed if more than three-fourths of the states agree to it. This was done so that small **groups couldn't just make changes** whenever they wanted.

205. **Since 1787, there have been twenty-seven amendments** added to the original document. Many of them give Americans more rights or expand on the original ones.

206. **The Constitution is the cornerstone of the United States.** It's what makes the nation a democracy. It also ensures that everyone has equal rights in the country.

207. **Although the US is not credited with inventing democracy,** it invented the kind of democracy we are familiar with today. The US is also the oldest continuous democracy in the world.

208. **The Constitution was revolutionary** when it was written and continues to be so today. Almost every nation in the world was not free when the Constitution was signed.

209. **Constitution Day is** celebrated on **September 17th**, the day it was signed.

210. In 1789, **George Washington** stated that **November 26th** would be a day of **thanksgiving for the Constitution**. It was the first time a president acknowledged the holiday of Thanksgiving.

The First President of the United States

This chapter will explore the life and legacy of George Washington, the first president of the United States. We'll look at thirty interesting facts about his early life, military career, political career, and retirement at Mount Vernon. Additionally, we'll learn some fun facts about the man himself!

211. **George Washington** was the first president of the United States. He served from **1789 to 1797**.

212. He is known as the **"Father of His Country."**

213. Washington's face appears on the **US one-dollar bill** and the quarter.

214. **George Washington was born in Virginia** on February 22nd, 1732, into a wealthy slave-holding family. He lived on a plantation called Mount Vernon.

215. He had no middle name. But he did have **three younger brothers**, two of which, John Augustine and Samuel, became officers in the American Revolutionary War. He also had other siblings and half-siblings.

216. At the age of eleven, Washington's formal schooling ended because his father died. Instead of going to England for an education, **he worked as a surveyor in the US** before joining the military just before the French and Indian War broke out.

217. **Washington was largely self-educated**. In 1744, he transcribed a manual about etiquette. Washington's exercise became known as **Rules of Civility & Decent Behavior in Company and Conversation.** It details advice on how one should act with others. It is believed these guidelines played a crucial role in how Washington conducted himself.

218. **Washington married Martha Dandridge Custis** when he was twenty-six years old. She brought two children from her previous marriage whom they raised together. **Washington had no biological children.**

219. **George Washington was one of America's Founding Fathers**. Other popular Founding Fathers include Thomas Jefferson, Benjamin Franklin, and John Adams.

220. **Washington was a crucial leader in the American Revolution**.

221. He is known **for crossing the Delaware River** with troops to take Trenton during the Revolutionary War due to a famous painting. The battle helped turn morale around.

222. He was **appointed commander in chief of the Continental Army** in 1775. He officially resigned from his position in December 1783.

223. In June 1787, **George Washington attended the Constitutional Convention**. He was nominated as its president. He presided over debates among delegates about how best to organize a new government for the United States of America.

224. In 1789, George Washington became **the first US president**.

225. During his presidency, **he set precedents that are still followed today.** For example, he appointed Cabinet members to advise him on policy decisions and formed an executive department. He gave the first State of the Union Address and **created diplomatic relations between the US and other countries.** Under his presidency, a national bank was created.

226. Almost six hundred slaves worked at Mount Vernon during his lifetime. **He eventually spoke out against slavery,** calling it "a reproach upon human nature." However, he never denounced the practice in public. He advocated for gradual emancipation rather than a sudden, drastic change that could lead to social unrest or revolt among freed slaves who had no means of support. George Washington freed all of his slaves in his will.

227. **He was a Freemason** and served as the Worshipful Master of his Lodge in Alexandria, Virginia. The Freemasons were a secret order that only men could join. They are still around today!

228. **Washington owned a large collection of books** on topics like philosophy, math, politics, and more.

229. **Washington only spoke English,** so he needed translators when dealing with colonists from foreign countries.

230. **George Washington was a founding member of the Society for Promoting Agriculture.** This organization encouraged people living in rural areas to become better farmers by sharing ideas about crop rotation methods and other farming techniques.

231. **He was a keen horseman** and owned many horses over his lifetime, even having some specially bred for racing.

232. **George Washington had false teeth made from ivory,** which were held together by springs. People tend to say he had wooden teeth, but that is a myth. His false teeth often caused him great pain while eating or speaking, so it wasn't unusual to see him without them.

233. **He loved fishing** and would go out regularly at Mount Vernon. Fish was his favorite food.

234. **Washington enjoyed drinking** and had several favorite alcoholic beverages. However, he drank in moderation, as he knew the effects of drinking too much alcohol in one sitting.

235. **Washington was unanimously elected for a second term.** He retired from office at the age of sixty-five after serving two terms as president. He set a precedent. The only person to serve more than two terms was Franklin Delano Roosevelt. After Roosevelt died, an amendment created a two-term limit on the presidency.

236. **When Washington first became president,** there were only thirteen states. By the end of his life, there were sixteen states in the Union.

237. **Washington's** Farewell Address in 1796 warned Americans to stay away from foreign entanglements and to **avoid the formation of political parties**. He also advised against the accumulation of debt by individuals and governments.

238. **After his presidency, he moved back to Mount Vernon,** where he spent the rest of his life overseeing business operations at the plantation. He also cultivated wheat for export. He died on December 14th, 1799, from an illness related to a throat infection.

239. **George Washington is consistently listed as one of the best US presidents**. He was known for his integrity, honesty, and strong leadership skills. His qualities earned him great respect from both sides of the political divide during America's early days as a young nation.

240. **In 1885, Congress created an annual holiday named after Washington to recognize all that he had achieved as president.** Initially, the holiday was celebrated on Washington's birthday. The date was later changed to the third Monday of February and morphed into Presidents' Day.

The War of 1812

This chapter will explore the history and key elements of **the War of 1812**. This war was fought between **the United States and Great Britain.** With these thirty facts, you'll discover how this conflict helped solidify US independence from British rule. We'll also learn **about American heroes**, such as **Andrew Jackson and Oliver Hazard Perry**, who led battles during this war. Discover the important outcomes resulting from the War of 1812, including a boundary line still in place today.

241. The War of 1812 was fought between t**he United States and Great Britain.**

242. It lasted for two years and eight months, **from June 1812 to February 1814.**

243. Both sides were trying to gain more control over territories in **North America and at sea.**

244. The impressment of sailors was a big problem. The British would forcefully **recruit US sailors to serve on British ships.**

245. **The US was also upset over the British blockade of France.** America was a new nation and needed trading partners to sustain itself. **The Napoleonic Wars were in full swing in Europe.** It became clear that America could not remain neutral, especially when France blockaded Britain.

246. On June 18th, 1812, **President James Madison** signed the declaration of war.

247. **Britain was busy fighting France in Europe** at the start of the war. It sent around five thousand people at the beginning of the war. By the end of the war, almost fifty thousand men were fighting.

248. **The US had around seven thousand soldiers at the start of the war.** By the end, nearly thirty-six thousand men were engaged in conflicts.

249. **The War of 1812 largely took place in Canada,** although several key battles happened in the Great Lakes region of the US.

250. The first battle in the war was **the siege of Fort Mackinac in July 1812.** "Battle" might be too strong a word. The soldiers on Mackinac Island, Michigan, didn't even know the war had broken out. They surrendered to the British without a fight.

251. **Many Native Americans fought alongside the British during the war.** After the war ended, they realized Britain would no longer help shield them from the influx of settlers heading west.

252. **Tecumseh was a Shawnee chief who led a confederacy of tribes.** He aided the British during the war and was instrumental in taking Fort Detroit from the US.

253. **Tecumseh died during the Battle of the Thames in October 1813.** His death caused the confederacy to fragment.

254. **General Andrew Jackson led some of the American forces in the war.** He won crucial victories, such as the Battle of New Orleans in January 1815. This battle was actually fought after the peace treaty had been signed overseas.

255. **Jackson would later become the president.** And he was not the only future president that fought in the War of 1812. John Quincy Adams, James Monroe, and William Henry Harrison also fought in this war.

256. **At the beginning of the war, the US Navy only had sixteen ships!** It had hundreds of smaller vessels, though. The British navy was much larger, but it also had the Napoleonic Wars to deal with in Europe.

257. **The US Navy experienced great success in the War of 1812.** The British Royal Navy was considered the best in the world, but the US Navy defeated the British in several key battles, such as the Battle of Lake Erie in September 1813.

258. **Commodore Oliver Hazard Perry led the US Navy to victory at the Battle of Lake Erie.** The US held control over the lake for the rest of the war. This win allowed them to win the Battle of the Thames and end Tecumseh's confederacy. The US was also able to take back Fort Detroit.

259. **In August 1814, the British set fire to the White House, the Capitol,** and other buildings. First Lady Dolley Madison is believed to have saved the portrait of George Washington, which still hangs in the White House to this day.

260. **Four days later, a huge storm and a tornado** swept through the area, extinguishing the flames. Although the weather put the fires out, it also caused more destruction.

261. During the war, **Francis Scott** Key wrote a poem called **"Defence of Fort M'Henry."** The poem turned into the lyrics for "The Star-Spangled Banner," which later became the US national anthem.

262. He wrote the poem after witnessing the **Battle of Baltimore,** which was fought in September 1814. The poem has four stanzas. The first stanza is the one that is commonly sung today.

263. Although neither side achieved an overall victory, it became known as **the Second War of Independence** because it solidified US independence from British rule.

264. **The Treaty of Ghent** was signed in December 1814, officially ending the war. Since neither side had technically won, the treaty restored the "status quo ante bellum" (meaning both sides agreed to return any land or goods captured during the war).

265. **The Treaty of Ghent** established a boundary line between Canada and the US. This line still exists today.

266. **After the war, American trade with Britain increased.** More settlers came to America looking for new land and a new life.

267. **The period after the war saw rapid growth in America's industry and economy** due to improved trade relations with Britain and other European countries.

268. **The War of 1812 also helped to shape the country's military and naval forces.** For instance, Winfield Scott introduced a training system that improved the US Army's performance.

269. Many monuments dedicated to those who served or died during this conflict still stand today **to remind us of what they achieved** for future generations.

270. **The War of 1812** helped forge a more robust national identity and increased pride in being an American.

The Indian Removal Act and the Trail of Tear

This chapter will explore the Indian Removal Act and its devastating impact on Native American tribes in the United States. We'll look at how this act led to forced relocations and the **Trail of Tears**, a long journey that saw thousands suffer hardships.

271. **The Indian Removal Act** was passed by US Congress **on May 28th, 1830,** during the presidency of Andrew Jackson.

272. **The act forcibly removed Native Americans from their lands** east of the Mississippi River. They were to be relocated to lands west of the river that had been acquired through treaties with other tribes.

273. **President Andrew Jackson** is widely regarded as one of the main figures responsible for passing the Indian Removal Act and authorizing its implementation. The act did have opposition from Congress members like **Henry Clay, Daniel Webster, and Davy Crockett.**

274. **Jackson believed removal was the best way to grow the American economy.** He said getting rid of the Native Americans would allow states like Alabama and Mississippi "to advance rapidly in population, wealth, and power."

275. After the passage of the Indian Removal Act, many **Native American leaders tried to resist removal** by appealing directly to the US Supreme Court. They also petitioned President Jackson himself, although their pleas fell on deaf ears.

276. **In 1832, the Supreme Court declared that the "Indian Nations" were separate nations** and that the US needed to treat the Native Americans as it would any other nation. Although the ruling was never enforced, it did lay the foundations for tribal sovereignty.

277. **More than forty-six thousand Native Americans were forced to leave their ancestral homes due to this act.** The five main tribes the Indian Removal Act affected were the **Cherokee, Muscogee (Creek), Choctaw, Seminole, and Chickasaw.**

278. These people embarked on a journey known as the **Trail of Tears.** They traveled over five thousand miles, although the amount the Native Americans traveled depended on where they lived.

279. The trail went across rugged terrain. **The Native Americans endured harsh conditions with little food** or supplies provided by the federal government agents who were assigned to oversee their relocation process.

280. **The number of deaths on the Trail of Tears is not known.** It is estimated that at least ten thousand Native Americans died during this long trek due to exhaustion, malnutrition, disease, and exposure.

281. **The Cherokees alone suffered at least four thousand deaths.** The death toll goes as high as six thousand.

282. **John Ross was the chief of the Cherokee.** He was one-eighth Cherokee, but he grew up with the Cherokees. The Cherokees are matrilineal, and his mother was Cherokee. He fought hard for the Cherokee to remain in their homeland. His wife died on the trail.

283. **Most Native Americans traveled on foot,** although some traveled by boat, in wagons, or on horseback.

284. **The Trail of Tears took place for several years.** People were removed from the Southeast from 1830 to 1850.

285. **The Indian Removal Act led to a war**. The Second Seminole War was fought because the US had voided a previous treaty with the passing of the act. The Seminoles were defeated in this war.

286. After removal, **the property** previously held **by Native Americans** was confiscated and **given to white settlers** or taken by the government.

287. This period in history remains controversial to this day. **It led to great suffering for Native Americans** and their families, many of whom were forced from their homes at gunpoint.

288. **Despite this hardship, some Native Americans resisted removal through legal means.** Others used guerrilla tactics, such as sabotage or escape attempts, when confronted with US troops.

289. **The Indian Removal Act did not remove all of the Native Americans from the Southeast**. For instance, some eluded the US Army and melted into the backwoods of the Southeast. Some Cherokee were allowed to stay in North Carolina after assisting the US Army.

290. Those who were removed **lived on established reservations, which were mostly located in Oklahoma.** The land was different from what they had been used to, and they also had to deal with other tribes already living there.

291. **Today, there are around five million Native Americans in the US.** About 30 percent of them live on reservations.

292. **The Indian Removal Act** had far-reaching consequences. Native American communities on either side of the Mississippi River have experienced economic disparities and land disputes for generations.

293. It is not known for sure where the name **"Trail of Tears"** came from. The name was first printed in 1908.

294. **The Indian Removal Act was repealed in 1980.**

295. **The Trail of Tears National Historic Trail** was established in 1987. It stretches over nine states, from Georgia to Oklahoma and north to Illinois.

296. **The trail is a memorial for those who lost their lives.** It also serves as a reminder that the US government's policy toward Native Americans has not always been fair.

297. **The trail** preserves critical cultural sites along the route, such as burial grounds, villages, and sacred places.

298. **Every year, many people visit parts of the original path** that Native Americans were forced to take when they were forcibly removed from their homes.

299. **Many Native American activists have condemned the Indian Removal Act** over the years. Historians have also looked down on the act due to its devastating impact on indigenous populations.

300. **The Indian Removal Act was also seen as a violation** of several treaties signed between the US government and tribes. The treaties were supposed to protect their rights but led to their displacement without compensation or adequate protection.

The Civil War

This chapter will explore **the history of the Civil War**, a conflict that lasted from 1861 to 1865. Over three million soldiers fought for their beliefs. We'll take a look at thirty interesting facts about how the **North (the Union) and the South (the Confederacy)** fought one another, what strategies were employed by both sides, and why the South decided to secede from the Union in the first place. Additionally, we'll examine the impact this had on African Americans who gained freedom during this period.

301. **The Civil War was fought between 1861 and 1865** in the United States of America.

302. It was a war **between the North** (the Union) **and the South** (the Confederacy).

303. The leading cause of the **war was slavery,** as many disagreed on whether it should be allowed.

304. **Abraham Lincoln became president** in 1860 and was inaugurated (entered office) in 1861.

305. Although **Lincoln** never expressed a desire to abolish slavery outright, the South was worried the new Republican government might do that. Before Lincoln was inaugurated, seven **Southern states had already left the Union.**

306. On February 8th, 1861, the **Confederate States of America was officially founded**. In total, eleven states seceded from the Union.

307. The first battle of **the Civil War** occurred at **Fort Sumter** in South Carolina in April 1861 when Confederates fired upon US troops stationed there. No one died from the fighting, and the US evacuated the fort.

308. **The First Battle of Bull Run took place in Virginia** on July 21st, 1861. The Union expected an easy victory; the Confederates won the day. Thomas J. Jackson earned his famous nickname, "Stonewall," in this battle for holding the line.

309. **The Battle of Shiloh,** which took place in northern Tennessee in 1862, saw approximately twenty-three thousand casualties in just two days, making it one of the bloodiest battles of **the Civil War.**

310. **The Battle of Antietam** occurred in September 1862 in Maryland. Prior to this battle, **the Confederacy had just scored an important victory** at the Second Battle of Bull Run and expected another win. The Union was able to repel the Confederacy's invasion of the North.

311. **The Battle of Antietam** paved the way for President Lincoln to issue his famous Emancipation Proclamation in January 1863. It freed all slaves in the "rebellious states." The border states (slave states that did not secede) were not affected by the Emancipation Proclamation.

312. In July 1863, one of the most important battles of the Civil War took place: **the Battle of Gettysburg.** This battle is seen as the turning point in the war. **The Union stopped any Confederate** plans of invasion and put the Confederates on the defensive.

313. The famous Pickett's Charge was ordered by Confederate **General Robert E. Lee.** He wanted to break through the Union lines at Gettysburg, but it failed and cost thousands of casualties. Gettysburg was the bloodiest battle in the war.

314. **Abraham Lincoln** gave his memorable Gettysburg Address about four months after the Union victory at that battle site, cementing its place in history.

315. In 1862, **Congress passed an act that freed enslaved people whose masters fought for the South.** African American volunteers joined the Union Army in droves. Almost 180,000 African Americans served in the army, while 19,000 served in the navy.

316. **Women played an essential role on both sides.** Nurses like Clara Barton helped wounded soldiers at battlefield hospitals and held fundraisers for relief efforts.

317. **Both sides used new naval technology,** such as ironclad ships and submarines. Ironclad ships were used for war for the first time in the US Civil War. And a Confederate submarine was the first submarine to sink an enemy ship.

318. **The Civil War** also saw the introduction of new weapons, such as new versions of repeating rifles like the Spencer rifle and Gatling guns. These weapons would change the face of warfare forever.

319. **Generals William Sherman and Philip Sheridan** are famous for their scorched-earth policy, which saw them burn down villages in the South to deprive Confederate troops of shelter and supplies.

320. On April 9th, 1865, **General Robert E. Lee** surrendered at Appomattox Court House, marking an end to hostilities between the North and South.

321. **Approximately 620,000 soldiers died** during the four years of fighting. The Civil War is considered to be the bloodiest war in US history.

322. Following the defeat, **some Confederates fled across the border into Mexico and Brazil,** where they formed communities known as Confederados.

323. **President Lincoln** was assassinated on April 14th, 1865, shortly after winning reelection for a second term and shortly after the Civil War ended.

324. After Lincoln's death, **Andrew Johnson** became president and oversaw the Reconstruction efforts. He also granted pardons to many former Confederates who had fought against Union forces.

325. **The Reconstruction era** began shortly after the war's conclusion and lasted until 1877, when US government troops withdrew from former Confederate states.

326. **After four years of war,** many cities and towns were destroyed throughout the South. It would take decades for some to rebuild.

327. **The Thirteenth Amendment was passed in 1865,** officially outlawing slavery throughout the United States of America.

328. **In 1866, Congress passed the Fourteenth Amendment**, which gave former slaves the same rights as listed in the Bill of Rights. The amendment did not apply to women of any race.

329. **In 1869, the Fifteenth Amendment was passed.** This amendment protected voting rights for black males.

330. **Today, it is debated how much the Reconstruction helped the country.** The country was put back together after the war, but African Americans still faced discrimination and segregation. Things would not start to get better for them until the 1960s.

The Old West

This chapter will explore **the history of life in the Old West between 1865 and 1895**. We'll take a look at thirty interesting facts about what happened during this iconic time period, such as **the gold rushes, famous outlaws** who earned their notoriety through daring **heists and robberies**, details on how **cowboys lived** while herding cattle on long journeys, and more! Discover famous chiefs like **Sitting Bull,** who fought bravely against US forces and other important aspects of life out west that helped shape the US into what it is today!

331. **The Old West** was a period in the United States between 1865 and 1895.

332. **Cowboys were men** who herded cattle on long journeys called cattle drives. They also did other things, such as care for horses and repair fences.

333. **Cattle drives took cowboys** months to complete. They often faced danger along the way from rustlers trying to steal their cattle!

334. Other dangers like mountain lions, rattlesnakes, wolves, and bears lurked around every corner, so **cowboys needed to be careful** while out on the range.

335. **Cowboys slept under the stars.** They also carried a canvas tent with them in case the weather didn't cooperate.

336. **Cowboys wore big hats** that kept the sun off their faces while herding cattle during long days in hot or rainy weather.

337. **Cowboys ate a lot of beans and beef** while herding cattle. They also ate hard biscuits and dried fruit. Coffee was their preferred beverage.

338. **Buffalo Bill Cody** held the first big rodeo in 1882. In rodeos, people could show off their skills by roping calves or riding wild horses. These events attracted large crowds of spectators looking for entertainment of a different kind.

339. **Gunslingers were expert marksmen who could shoot accurately**, sometimes even from horseback. Sharpshooting became very popular during this time. Buffalo Bill even made a traveling show involving fancy gun tricks and plays. His shows starred **Annie Oakley, Sitting Bull, and Wild Bill Hickok.**

340. **People who moved west faced a lot of challenges.** Getting to their new home was difficult, as everything had to be moved by wagon. And once the new family got there, they had to build a cabin and barn and then plant crops. And that was on top of other chores, like cooking, cleaning, and repairing items.

341. **Life was hard on the frontier.** There were few stores or doctors, so one had to be prepared for anything that could happen.

342. **Wells Fargo** was an important mail delivery service established in California in 1852. It used stagecoaches instead of horseback riders for long distances.

343. **The Pony Express** was a way to send letters and news across the country. It was established in 1860. Riders would **travel on horseback while carrying mail** for long distances. Pony Express stations would provide a place to rest, eat, and get a fresh horse for the next leg of the trip.

344. **The Transcontinental Railroad** was built between 1863 and 1869. It connected the eastern states of America with California, which made it much easier for people to travel westward.

345. **Settlers also ran into problems with Native Americans,** who had lived off the land long before settlers arrived. The tribes hunted, farmed, fished, and gathered food in the West.

346. The influx of settlers led to clashes with the Native Americans. US forces were called in to fight Native Americans. **The tribes were upset the settlers were taking away their land** and hunting buffalo to near extinction.

347. **Millions of buffalo once roamed freely in large herds in the West,** but as settlers moved westward, they killed them for food and sport. The buffalo also suffered from disease and drought.

348. In 1889, there were less than **six hundred buffalo left in the Great Plains.**

349. **Native Americans formed powerful alliances** as settlers continued moving westward. Chiefs like **Sitting Bull fought against US forces** to protect their people.

350. **Sitting Bull was a Hunkpapa Lakota leader.** He led the native forces against Lieutenant Colonel George Custer in the Battle of the Little Bighorn. Everyone in Custer's battalion died.

351. **Crazy Horse also fought in the Battle of the Little Bighorn**, which took place in 1876. Crazy Horse is most remembered for his tragic death. He was killed by a US soldier after resisting arrest. To this day, it is not known for sure if he ever resisted.

352. **Buffalo Soldiers were African American cavalry** units of the US Army who fought in many battles against Native Americans and protected settlers during westward expansion. The American Indian Wars started long before the time of the Old West and would not end until the 1920s.

353. **The discovery of gold** in states like California, Montana, and Colorado led many people to travel westward to become wealthy, displacing Native Americans in the process.

354. People from all over the world came to take part in these **gold rushes**. Around sixty-seven thousand **Chinese immigrated to California** during the gold rush years.

355. **Towns grew quickly** as more people moved westward to look for land, adventure, and wealth. More than 300,000 people moved to California during the gold rush!

356. **Sheriffs kept law and order in towns** by arresting criminals or outlaws, sometimes with help from deputies or even posses that tracked down wanted men!

357. **Vigilante justice was common in the Wild West**. Law enforcement couldn't keep up with criminals, so posses would hunt down wanted men, sometimes without legal authority from a judge or jury of peers.

358. **Jesse James was a famous outlaw in the Old West**. He led men in the first daytime bank robbery during a time of peace.

359. Other famous outlaws include **Billy the Kid and Butch Cassidy and the Sundance Kid**.

360. **The Wild West** was full of **adventure, danger, and excitement**. It has been immortalized by books, movies, and television shows for generations to come.

The Industrial Revolution

This chapter will explore **the history and impact of the Industrial Revolution**. We'll look at thirty facts about how this period changed life in America and around the world, from new inventions that made production faster to advances in communication and transportation. **We'll also discuss how it sparked a population boom in cities** across America while creating new jobs and opportunities for people.

361. **The Industrial Revolution** began in the United States around 1790 and ended around 1870.

362. **During this period, many changes took place** to make production easier and faster. **New machines were invented,** which allowed people to produce more items in shorter amounts of time than ever before.

363. **Many new inventions during the Industrial Revolution made life easier for Americans.** Sewing machines could make clothes quicker, and cotton gins could separate fibers quickly so they could be made into textiles like clothing or blankets.

364. One crucial invention was **the steam engine, which allowed machines to be powered by steam.** The steam engine helped power factories in cities across America at unprecedented speeds.

365. With the help of these **new technologies,** industries started booming. Businesses flourished like never before!

366. **The Industrial Revolution** saw the rise of large-scale factories and production centers, allowing for the mass production of items. This was particularly important in developing textiles. Machines could produce more cloth faster than ever!

367. **Coal and iron ore mining also boomed during this period.** Coal fueled steam engines, and iron ore was needed to make steel.

368. **New industries emerged, such as steel** (which provided materials needed for buildings) and oil production (which powered new machines and vehicles).

369. **A big part of the Industrial Revolution was transportation**. New roads were built so goods could be transported quickly from one place to another. Steamships revolutionized sea travel. They were much faster than ships powered only by sails!

370. **New railroad tracks** made it possible for people to travel longer distances at greater speeds.

371. **The construction of the Erie Canal** finished in 1852. The canal connected the Atlantic Ocean to the Great Lakes, which cut the costs of transporting goods to the US interior.

372. **The telegraph also became widely available** during this time. Telegraphs allowed people to communicate over vast distances without waiting days or weeks for letters like they did before.

373. **Newspapers and magazines were also mass produced** and distributed during the Industrial Revolution. People could more easily be informed about worldwide events.

374. **Advances in medicine** helped reduce deaths from diseases. For instance, in 1800, Dr. Benjamin Waterhouse gave his children the first smallpox vaccine in the US. The vaccine had been developed four years earlier by an English doctor named Edward Jenner.

375. **Financial services grew rapidly** during this time due to increased demand from businesses looking for investments or loans. In 1790, the Philadelphia Stock Exchange became the first stock exchange in the US.

376. **The Industrial Revolution changed how**

Americans worked. It made everyday life easier for some while creating new jobs and opportunities.

377. However, **working conditions were not great** for those in the factories or coal mines. People worked in cramped spaces and dealt with heavy machinery.

378. Although the wealthy enjoyed the increase in goods, **poorer people worked twelve- to sixteen-hour days**, six days a week, just to scrape by.

379. **Children worked in factories** and coal mines as well. Their small fingers were perfect for working on delicate yet dangerous machinery.

380. Coal mining was a very dangerous job. **Mines could collapse unexpectedly**, and coal dust caused serious breathing problems.

381. **The newsies were young boys who sold newspapers** on the corners of busy streets. They were typically orphaned and were paid pennies for selling newspapers.

382. **Child labor laws** were eventually signed into law. For instance, the Cotton Factories Regulation Act of 1819 set the minimum working age to nine. Children in the textile industry could work up to twelve hours a day.

383. **Adult workers fought for their rights** in the workplace. They began forming unions, allowing them to fight for better working conditions, including higher pay or shorter hours.

384. **The American Federation of Labor** was formed by Samuel Gompers in 1886. Although it made some strides, working conditions for most Americans would not get better until the early 20th century.

385. **Women's roles also started changing.** They gained increased access to education, jobs outside the home, and even voting rights in some places.

386. **The US economy grew significantly** during the Industrial Revolution, creating new wealth through trade and industry.

387. It also led to a **population boom in cities** across America, with people flocking from rural areas in search of work opportunities.

388. **Immigration also increased** during this period. Many Europeans were attracted by the possibilities the growing American economy offered!

389. Some people were angry about the influx of immigrants. **Immigrants were willing to take a job with lower pay** and deal with poor working conditions. This led to much resentment.

390. The US had more than one Industrial Revolution. **The Second Industrial Revolution took off soon after the First Industrial Revolution ended.** The Third Industrial Revolution happened during the mid- to late 20th century. Some historians believe we are in the Fourth Industrial Revolution right now.

The Spanish-American War

This chapter will explore **the Spanish-American War,** a conflict between the United States and Spain that lasted from April to August 1898.

We'll look at thirty interesting facts about **how this war began** and why it's an important milestone in American history. Discover some fascinating facts about **Theodore Roosevelt's** volunteer cavalry unit and a journalist named **Richard Harding Davis**.

391. **The Spanish-American War** was a conflict between the United States and Spain that lasted from April to August 1898.

392. It began when an **American warship**, the USS Maine, blew up in Havana Harbor, Cuba, while on a diplomatic mission.

393. **Yellow journalism** (similar to modern-day tabloids) pointed the finger at Spain. Recent examinations have determined that the Maine exploded because something went wrong on the ship.

394. Over a month later, **President William McKinley asked Congress to declare war on Spain.** He wanted to support the Cuban rebels fighting for independence from Spanish control. The country was also still upset over the sinking of the Maine, with most people believing Spain was behind it.

395. **The US wanted to help Cuba gain its freedom.** There were also many US citizens living on the island. The US invested money in businesses in Cuba and relied on trade with it.

396. **The Spanish-American War was an important milestone in US history**, as it marked the first time that a large part of its military forces was used overseas.

397. **The Battle of Manila Bay** took place on May 1st, 1898. The Americans headed to the Philippines to ensure the Spanish naval forces there would not go to Cuba to aid in the war effort. The Spanish were crushed, ending their colonial rule over the islands.

398. **The Battle of San Juan Hill** occurred on July 1st, 1898. The Americans trounced the Spanish and practically ensured they would be the victors in Cuba.

399. Future **American president Theodore Roosevelt** led his volunteer cavalry unit known as the Rough Riders into battle at San Juan Hill near Santiago de Cuba. This helped solidify him as a national hero!

400. Although they were called the **Rough Riders**, only the officers rode horses into battle!

401. **The Buffalo Soldiers,** which were units comprised of African Americans, also served with distinction on the battlefield. Although they faced racial tensions at home, white commanders in the US Army praised the Buffalo Soldiers' bravery.

402. **The Battle of El Caney** happened on the same day as **the Battle of San Juan Hill**. The Americans technically won this battle, but El Caney did not prove useful to them, especially in light of the causalities they suffered.

403. On July 3rd, 1898, the Battle of Santiago de Cuba took place. **All of the Spanish ships were destroyed,** while the US Navy remained intact. This battle ended the Cuban theater of the war.

404. **The Spanish-American War had a large impact on journalism.** Richard Harding Davis became the first US war correspondent. He went to the front lines of the war in Cuba to give readers back home a better understanding of the events happening so far away.

405. **Davis was not the only journalist to travel

to the front lines.** Others traveled to Cuba as well to get the latest scoop.

406. Newspaper owners like **William Randolph Hearst** and **Joseph Pulitzer** competed to see who could sell the most papers.

407. Around **three thousand Americans died in the war,** although most of those deaths were from yellow fever. It is not known for certain how many Spanish died, but the best estimate is between fifty-five thousand and sixty thousand.

408. **The war ended with the signing of the Treaty of Paris,** which was signed in December 1898.

409. **The treaty gave America control over Cuba**. Spain ceded Guam, Puerto Rico, and the Philippines to the US.

410. **The US occupied Cuba** until the Republic of Cuba was formed in 1902.

411. **Although the US left Cuba in 1902**, it ensured it would still have a say in Cuban politics. In 1903, the Platt Amendment was passed, allowing the US to interfere with international and domestic Cuban affairs if it impacted the island's independence.

412. **The Treaty of Paris of 1898** stated that the US would pay twenty million dollars for the acquisition of the Philippines.

413. **The Philippine-American War** would break out in February 1902 because the Filipinos sought their independence, not another ruling colonial power.

414. The war would last for over **fourteen years** and end in an American victory.

415. The **Philippines** would be granted its independence after World War II.

416. **Guam and Puerto Rico are still US possessions today.**

417. **The Spanish-American War** is seen as the beginning of an American empire, although the US has never announced its designs on creating an empire.

418. As a result of the war, **Spain no longer had possessions in the Western Hemisphere.** The Spanish Empire was officially on the decline.

419. About ten years after the war, **the Great White Fleet,** an impressive collection of sixteen battleships painted all white, sailed around the world to demonstrate America's growing naval power.

420. **New technologies were being developed** around the time of the Spanish-American War, such as machine guns, improved naval ships, and larger-scale military maneuvers. This allowed enemies to be defeated much more quickly, leading to a new era of warfare seen during the world wars.

World War One

This chapter will explore **the history of World War One**. We'll take a look at thirty interesting facts about how America became involved in the conflict and what it brought to the European war effort.

We'll also learn about advances in technology and the development of new tactics like trench warfare and submarine attacks.

421. **World War I began in Europe on July 28th, 1914,** and ended with an armistice signed on November 11th, 1918.

422. The war began for several reasons, but the main trigger was the assassination of **Franz Ferdinand on June 28th, 1914**, by a Bosnian Serb radical.

423. **The United States joined the war** after Germany attacked several American ships carrying goods to England in 1917.

424. **The Zimmermann Note** was another reason the US decided to declare war.

425. This was a **secret piece of German intelligence** sent to Mexico in early 1917. The note said that if the US entered the war, **Germany would enter into an alliance with Mexico** and help it retrieve territories it had lost to the US. The telegram was intercepted and led to outrage in the US.

426. **President Woodrow Wilson declared war against Germany on April 6th, 1917**, for their attack on American ships at sea and violations of US neutrality rights.

427. In May 1917, **Wilson signed a bill introducing military conscription**, otherwise known as "the draft."

428. Over **four million Americans served in the military** during World War I.

429. **The first American soldiers** to fight on European soil during WWI arrived in France on June 26th, 1917.

430. **African American soldiers** made up 13 percent of the US forces during WWI. They fought for their country but had limited rights back home.

431. **Women served as nurses** in the armed forces during WWI but not as officers or enlisted personnel until WWII.

432. **The Allies in Europe were exhausted from the fighting.** The conflicts were harsh and bloody. The arrival of the US soldiers greatly boosted morale.

433. Perhaps the most well-known **aspect of WWI was trench warfare.** Instead of fighting in the open, the soldiers in Europe dug trenches and fought from there.

434. **The trenches provided some safety,** but disease ran rampant. The main killer of the men in the trenches was artillery fire from the enemy. Debris from the blast could hit men who were close by, causing fatal wounds.

435. **Chemical warfare was used in WWI,** with the most popular being mustard gas. The US did not produce any chemical weapons during the war.

436. **During World War One, aviation played an important role** in military operations. By the end of the war, almost thirty-three thousand men had been enlisted to fly in aviation missions.

437. **The US Air Force was not around during World War One.** It was created after World War II.

438. **Submarines were used much more significantly** than in the past. A lot of "firsts" for submarines happened during World War One, such as the first submarine to sink a ship with a self-propelled torpedo and the first true submarine (submarines that were fully submerged in the water).

439. **The US government issued war bonds** to help fund their involvement in WWI. Money from these bonds went toward purchasing weapons and other necessary supplies for troops overseas, among other things.

440. **The United States Food Administration**, which was led by Herbert Hoover, made sure enough food was available at home and abroad throughout the war effort.

441. **America's involvement caused rapid growth in industry.** War production increased employment opportunities, especially for women at home.

442. **WWI had a significant impact on industrial production in the United States.** Manufacturers and producers moved away from producing consumer goods and focused more on war production, such as munitions, weapons, and other military equipment.

443. This resulted in an **increased demand for raw materials,** which led to the rapid expansion of the nation's industrial sector and a surge in industrial employment.

444. **The United States** participated in several battles, such as Château-Thierry, Belleau Wood, Saint-Mihiel, and the Meuse-Argonne Forest offensive.

445. **In November 1918, President Wilson set forth his Fourteen Points**, which proposed a new international system of peace and security for all nations after World War I.

446. **On November 11th, 1918, Germany signed an armistice with the Allied forces, ending WWI in Europe.**

447. **The Treaty of Versailles** was signed on June 28th, 1919, by representatives from 32 countries. This treaty marked the official end of World War One.

448. **An estimated twenty million soldiers died in WWI,** making it one of the deadliest wars in history. The US was only in the war for a little over a year. The other countries fought for over four years.

449. **More than 116,000 Americans died during WWI.**

450. **After the war, the Spanish flu broke out.** Around 675,000 people died of the flu. Contrary to the name, the Spanish flu didn't originate in Spain. Researchers believe it started in the state of Kansas.

The Women's Suffrage Movement

This chapter will explore the **history of the women's suffrage movement** and how it impacted life in the United States.

We'll take a look at **thirty facts** about this important movement, including its origins, leaders, key events, and victories.

451. **The fight for women's voting rights** in the United States began in 1848 at a convention held in Seneca Falls, New York.

452. **The Seneca Falls Convention** was the first organized gathering of people dedicated to fighting for women's rights and is often considered the start of the women's suffrage movement.

453. More than three hundred men and women gathered to hear people speak about **the suffrage movement.** One hundred of them signed the Declaration of Sentiments, which declared **"all men and women are created equal."**

454. There were earlier **fighters for women's rights,** such as **Mary Wollstonecraft**, who wrote books about how women were not inferior to men in the 18th century. She believed if women could have proper education, they could achieve great things.

455. **Elizabeth Cady Stanton** and **Lucretia Mott** were two crucial leaders during the Seneca Falls Convention. They spoke out against gender inequality and worked to establish voting rights for all citizens.

456. **The American Equal Rights Association** was founded in 1866. It fought for the right to vote, no matter one's gender or race.

457. **Many suffragists** were abolitionists and fought for the end of slavery.

458. When **the Fifteenth Amendment was proposed**, some suffragists were upset because there was no mention of women.

459. **Susan B. Anthony** and **Elizabeth Cady** Stanton protested the amendment and formed an organization called the National Woman Suffrage Association in 1869. This move caused a rift in the women's rights movement.

460. **The American Woman Suffrage Association (AWSA)** was founded in 1869 by Lucy Stone and focused on winning voting rights at the state level. It promoted black and women's suffrage.

461. By 1890, the suffrage movement had worked out their differences and combined to form **the National American Woman Suffrage Association.**

462. **The women's suffrage movement** brought together people from all walks of life. Wealthy white women were able to dedicate the most time, but poor women also joined the cause.

463. **African American suffragists like Ida B. Wells and Sojourner Truth** fought for their rights and those of other oppressed groups.

464. **Many men fiercely opposed the movement.** Women also joined anti-suffragist movements. Before 1916, more women joined anti-suffragist movements than suffragist organizations.

465. **Many brave women risked arrest** when they participated in protests demanding equal rights. For instance, **Susan B. Anthony** was arrested in 1872 for voting in an election.

466. **Suffragists created leaflets and newspapers** to spread their message and organized marches in cities all over the United States.

467. **In addition to voting rights**, suffragists fought for other women's rights, such as access to higher education, better working conditions, and labor laws that would protect them from discrimination based on gender. Some groups also advocated against discrimination of race.

468. In 1913, **Alice Paul and Lucy Burns** led **the first women's rights parade in DC.** Thousands of people marched through the capital, demanding voting rights for women.

469. **During World War I,** many suffragists campaigned hard for the right to vote. Woodrow Wilson publicly announced his support for women's suffrage in 1918, becoming the first president to do so.

470. **Women played an essential role in WWI.** Many historians believe their aid in the war effort led the vast majority of women to realize they deserved the right to vote..

471. **Jeannette Rankin from Montana** was the first woman elected into Congress in 1916, four years before the Nineteenth Amendment took effect in 1920.

472. **The Nineteenth Amendment** was passed in 1919 and ratified in 1920. It stated, "The right of citizens of the United States to vote shall not be denied or abridged by the United States or any State on account of sex."

473. The Nineteenth Amendment is sometimes referred to as **the Susan B. Anthony Amendment** due to her tireless work and dedication toward women's rights.

474. **Several states already allowed women to vote before 1920,** such as Arkansas, New York, Michigan, and Oklahoma, just to name a few.

475. **The League of Women Voters was formed in 1920.** It succeeded the National American Woman Suffrage Association. Instead of fighting for the right to vote, the League of Women Voters seeks to educate people about upcoming elections. It registers voters and promotes voting rights, as well as other issues.

476. **The Equal Rights Amendment** was proposed in 1923, but it wasn't approved by Congress until 1972. The ERA prohibits discrimination based on gender and would invalidate outdated laws regarding women.

477. **The ERA** did not receive enough votes for ratification, even after the deadline was extended to 1982. In 2020, Virginia ratified the ERA. If Congress decides to adopt the amendment, it will become the Twenty-eighth Amendment to the Constitution.

478. In 2020, **Kamala Harris** became the first female vice president of the United States. This historic moment would not have been possible without the suffrage movement, which allowed women full citizenship and voting rights.

479. As of today, **women in countries all over the world can vote, except in Vatican** City, which only allows the College of Cardinals to vote for the leader (the pope).

480. Although women can vote around the world, **women still face discrimination** and voting restrictions in many countries.

The Roaring Twenties

This chapter will explore **the Roaring Twenties**, a decade of **economic growth** and excitement **in the United States**.

Discover thirty interesting facts about popular music, new inventions, and Prohibition. Meet other iconic figures who made their mark during this time period, like **Babe Ruth** and **Al Capone**!

481. **The Roaring Twenties lasted from 1920 to 1929**. It was a period of economic growth and prosperity.

482. **Automobiles became more affordable** for middle-class Americans. At the beginning of 1920, there were eight million drivers. That number nearly tripled by the end of the decade!

483. **Many famous brands** that we know and love today first appeared in the 1920s, such as Wonder Bread, Kool-Aid, Rubbermaid, and Reese's peanut butter cups.

484. **Television was invented** in the 1920s but wouldn't become popular until after WWII.

485. **The first commercial radio news program** in the US aired in 1920. Radios grew in popularity during the Roaring Twenties. People could sit at home and listen to music, variety shows, and the news.

486. **Scientists discovered insulin** in 1921. It was first used in the US in 1922. Before this discovery, people with severe diabetes typically only lived for a few months at most.

487. **The first transatlantic telephone call** was made between the president of AT&T, Walter Gifford, and the head of the British post office, Evelyn Murray, in 1927.

488. **The first crossword puzzle book** was published in 1924 by Simon & Schuster, increasing the popularity of this activity.

489. **The Scopes Trial occurred in 1925** when John T. Scopes was accused of violating Tennessee state law. Scopes taught evolution in his classroom. He was ultimately found guilty, although the verdict was overturned.

490. **Women gained the right to vote** with the ratification of the Nineteenth Amendment in 1920.

491. **Women began working outside the home** in larger numbers than ever before. They attended college and enjoyed more freedom.

492. **Flappers were stylish young women** who wore their hair short. They enjoyed dancing, drinking alcohol, smoking cigarettes, and wearing makeup and short skirts. They went against the idea of how a proper woman should dress and act.

493. **Women's fashion changed significantly** during this time. Hemlines rose to above the knee, and new fabrics became available.

494. **The Art Deco style of architecture** and design defined the look of this era with its bold geometric shapes and bright colors.

495. **People enjoyed new dances** like the Charleston and the Lindy Hop at parties and nightclubs across the country.

496. Fads like **flagpole** sitting and **marathon dancing** became popular among young adults looking for excitement.

497. **The Harlem Renaissance** was a period of great cultural and artistic expression for African Americans.

498. Some well-known **African American** authors include Zora Neale Hurston, Langston Hughes, and Claude McKay.

499. **Jazz music** became popular in the United States, with musicians like Louis Armstrong and Duke Ellington leading the way.

500. **The Ku Klux Klan**, a violent hate group, grew in size throughout this decade due to anti-immigration sentiment. The KKK in the 1920s believed that native Protestant whites should be the ones to live in the US. Although the KKK was initially founded in the South, it became very popular in the Midwest during this time.

501. **Working conditions began to improve** during the 1920s. In 1926, Ford introduced the five-day workweek.

502. **Charles Lindbergh** became the first man to fly a solo, non-stop across the Atlantic Ocean in 1927. He flew his plane called the Spirit of St. Louis.

503. Charles Lindbergh is also well known for the **kidnapping of his son** in 1932, sparking a nationwide search for him. The baby was killed, although theories abound on who really killed him.

504. **Babe Ruth** broke baseball records, including hitting sixty home runs in one season. He became one of America's most beloved athletes!

505. **In 1926, American Gertrude Ederle** swam across the English Channel, becoming the first woman ever to do so. She was an Olympic champion and held multiple world records. She was one of many female sports heroes in the 1920s.

506. **Prohibition began when Congress ratified the Eighteenth Amendment** in 1919, banning alcohol production and distribution within US borders.

507. **Speakeasies sold liquor illegally.** They became popular during the Roaring '20s. In the late 1920s, there were around thirty-two thousand speakeasies in New York alone!

508. **Al Capone became one of America's most notorious gangsters** during this time. He was part of the bootlegging business, which means he illegally distributed alcohol to speakeasies. Capone led an organized crime syndicate out of Chicago.

509. On October 24th, 1929, **the American stock market crashed**. This day, which is known as Black Thursday, marked the highest number of sold shares in US history. On Black Tuesday (October 29th, 1929), the stock market crashed again, with investors trading millions of shares in just one day.

510. **The stock market crash marks the end of the Roaring Twenties** and the start of **the Great Depression.**

The Great Depression

This chapter will explore **the history of the Great Depression in the United States**. We'll look at thirty interesting facts about how this period of economic hardship began, what it meant for people living through it, and how various government initiatives attempted to alleviate suffering during this difficult time.

Learn about **new forms of entertainment** that developed during this era and other issues, such as **migration patterns** and **labor rights.**

511. **The Great Depression** was a time of **economic hardship** in the United States that lasted from 1929 to 1939.

512. It began after the **stock market crashed** on October 29th, 1929, which was known as Black Tuesday.

513. During this time, **millions lost their jobs and homes** due to business failures and bank closures.

514. It is believed that a third to **a half of all banks closed** during the Great Depression.

515. Nearly **25 percent of American workers were unemployed** in 1933.

516. Many homeless men, known as **hobos**, rode freight trains from city to city, **looking for work.**

517. **The Dust Bowl** further intensified the effects of the Depression on farmers in America's **Midwest and Great Plains.** Drought and severe dust storms damaged crops and people's health.

518. Many people **fled the regions affected by the Dust Bowl**. An estimated 2.5 million people moved out of the Great Plains by 1940.

519. To offset the effects of prolonged drought caused by the Dust Bowl, **the Soil Conservation Service** was established in 1935.

520. **Herbert Hoover** was the president from 1929 to 1933. He initially believed that economic recovery should be left to the private sector, but he eventually implemented programs and policies. Although some of his policies were sound, they took too much time to become useful.

521. One of the most iconic symbols of the Great Depression is **Hoovervilles**. Unemployed people built shantytowns that they named after the president.

522. **Crime increased** after the Great Depression, but it fell once successful programs were put in place.

523. In 1933, **the Twenty-first Amendment was ratified.** It repealed the Eighteenth Amendment, which made Prohibition the law of the land.

524. Organized crime continued to be a problem even after the Twenty-first Amendment was passed. Instead of bootlegging, **crime syndicates turned to gambling and racketeering.**

525. **President Franklin D. Roosevelt** was elected in 1932 on a platform of relief and reform.

526. **With the New Deal and the Second New Deal**, FDR created employment opportunities for millions of Americans. These workers built infrastructure projects, such as roads and dams.

527. **The Tennessee Valley Authority** was formed in 1933. It provided hydroelectric power production and flood control to seven states.

528. **The Social Security Act** was passed in 1935, which provided financial security to older people.

529. **The Works Progress Administration** (WPA) put unemployed people back to work by providing jobs in construction.

530. **The WPA also employed** people who were involved in **art and theater,** ensuring that American culture could still grow during this trying time.

531. **Artists created works that reflected American hardships.** Some of the most famous artists of this period include photographers **Dorothea Lange** and **Walker Evans** and the painter **Jackson Pollack.**

532. Some people were inspired by self-help books like Think and Grow Rich, which stressed personal responsibility over government intervention during hard times.

533. Despite economic hardship, **baseball was a popular pastime.** The New York Yankees won a World Series Championship in 1932.

534. **Women had a more significant presence in the workforce during this era** due to necessity. Some women worked in factories. Many worked in the domestic sphere or took government or clerical jobs.

535. **Women also often took on the role of caregiver, providing care** for the elderly and children while their husbands worked. Women took on the responsibility of managing the household budget and finding ways to make ends meet.

536. **The Great Depression saw a drop in the birth rate** due to economic hardship and a lack of available resources.

537. **In 1935, President Roosevelt signed the National Labor Relations Act into law,** which gave laborers more rights, including freedom of collective bargaining with employers.

538. **The Fair Labor Standards Act was passed in 1938.** It set a national minimum wage and placed restrictions on child labor. **Many children worked** dangerous factory jobs.

539. Despite attempts at recovery from various government initiatives during the 1930s, **the US economy only fully recovered during WWII.**

540. **World War II significantly impacted the Great Depression in the US.** It provided a resurgence of economic activity, employment opportunities, and wages. Additionally, the war provided a large influx of capital, which allowed the government to fund public works and social welfare programs that helped create today's prosperous economy.

World War Two

This chapter will explore **the history of World War II,** one of the most devastating wars in human history. We'll take a look at thirty **interesting facts about why it started** and what its lasting impacts were.

Learn about battles that changed the course of history, the technology developed during this time, and the human cost of the war.

541. **World War II** was fought from **1939 to 1945** and involved over fifty countries, including **the United States of America, Britain, Japan, and Germany.**

542. **President Franklin Delano Roosevelt (FDR)** wanted to join the war, but he knew the public would not support the idea. Many believed they should not join a war that did not involve the US.

543. **In 1941, FDR signed the Lend-Lease Act.** The act allowed the United States to supply materials to Allies fighting the Axis (Germany, Italy, and Japan).

544. **The aid was given to the Allies for free.** The US spent a little over $50 billion (around $720 billion today) to help the Allies win the war.

545. **The United States supplied more tanks and aircraft** to the Allies than any other country in World War II.

546. **Japan's attack on Pearl Harbor, Hawaii,** on December 7th, 1941, led the United States to join WWII against the Axis powers.

547. **After the Japanese attacked** Pearl Harbor, **FDR issued Executive Order No. 9066,** allowing the military to place people of Japanese ancestry living on the West Coast to internment camps.

548. **Over sixteen million Americans served in the US Armed Forces** during WWII. Over 400,000 of them were killed in battle or died due to other causes, such as illness or injury.

549. **In 1940, Congress approved the Selective Training and Service Act.** It was the first peacetime draft in the US. When WWII broke out, the draft's terms were amended. Over ten million men had been drafted into military service by 1945.

550. More than one million African Americans served during WWII. The war also saw the first African American officers.

551. Beginning in 1942, **women began contributing in full force to the war** effort. They joined the Army Nurse Corps, Women's Auxiliary Corps (WAC), Marine reserves, and the Navy WAVES unit during WWII.

552. **During WWII, women began to take on traditionally more masculine roles.** Women worked in factories, shipyards, and mines. During the war, women ensured the US economy continued to flourish and created military equipment for the war effort.

553. During the war, the US public felt a sense of patriotism and the desire to aid in the war effort. **Food and gas were rationed**. People planted **"victory gardens"** to grow their own food. Propaganda films increased the people's need to support their country during the war.

554. In December 1943, **the Cairo Conference was held in Egypt** by three major Allied powers (the US, the UK, and China). The three powers agreed that Nazi Germany needed to be destroyed for the war to end. The Allies also needed Japan's unconditional surrender.

555. On June 6th, 1944 (D-Day), 133,000 Allied troops **landed on beaches at Normandy, France,** beginning Europe's liberation from Nazi Germany.

556. **General Dwight Eisenhower** was the supreme commander of the Allied forces in Europe. He was in charge of the successful **D-Day operation,** which turned the tide against the Germans. He would go on to become the president of the United States.

557. **The G.I. Bill** was passed in 1944. It provided returning veterans with funds to pursue college degrees or start businesses after the war ended.

558. **The Holocaust occurred during World War II**. Six million European Jews were murdered under the Nazi regime. Another five million other minorities and Soviet prisoners of war were killed by the Germans during the war.

559. **American soldiers liberated several concentration camps,** which was where Jews and other minorities were sent to work and die. One of the most infamous concentration camps they liberated was Dachau. Liberating these camps made the soldiers realize the true horror of the war.

560. **On April 12th, 1945, FDR** passed away from a cerebral hemorrhage at Warm Springs, Georgia, leaving **Vice President Harry S. Truman** to assume office as the thirty-third president of the United States.

561. **Eisenhower** accepted Germany's unconditional surrender ending WWII in Europe on May 7th, 1945.

562. **Although the war in Europe was over,** the war in the Pacific was still ongoing. **The US Navy played a huge role in the Pacific** theater, winning important battles like **the Battle of Midway** and **the Battle of Leyte Gulf.**

563. One of the more famous Pacific battles was **the Battle of Iwo Jima.** It was a brutal fight between US and Japanese forces on the Pacific island of Iwo Jima. The battle lasted from February 19th to March 26th, 1945. The US won this battle.

564. **The Manhattan Project** was a top-secret program by the US government to build the first atomic bomb. It was carried out by tens of thousands of scientists and engineers from 1939 to 1945. It didn't officially start until 1942, though.

565. On July 16th, 1945, the US performed the first successful **atomic bomb test** in New Mexico.

566. A little over a month later, on August 6th, 1945, an **atomic bomb** was dropped by US military forces **on Hiroshima, Japan.**

567. **When Japan didn't surrender,** US forces dropped another **atomic bomb on Nagasaki** three days later. It is difficult to know how many died because of the aftereffects of the bombs. Hundreds of thousands died because of radiation effects and from the blast itself.

568. On August 14th, 1945, **Japan announced its surrender.** On September 2nd, 1945, Japan signed the Instrument of Surrender, officially ending the war.

569. Almost **five hundred Medals of Honor** were awarded to American soldiers who fought during WWII. The Medal of Honor is the highest award a soldier can receive.

570. After **World War II ended in 1945,** the United Nations was founded to help maintain peace among countries.

The Cold War and the Space Race

This chapter will explore **the history of the Cold War and the Space Race.** We'll examine thirty interesting facts about how this period impacted global relations, space exploration, scientific breakthroughs, and more! Learn about important figures like **Neil Armstrong** and **Yuri Gagarin**, who played a major role in outer space exploration. We'll also discuss key moments like **the Cuban Missile Crisis** and the building of **the Berlin Wall.**

571. **After WWII ended in 1945,** people from all over Europe came to live in major American cities like New York, Chicago, and Los Angeles. These immigrants brought their cultures, which shaped future generations.

572. **The Cold War** was a period in history when tensions escalated between the democratic **United States** and the communist **Soviet Union.**

573. **The Cold War lasted from 1945 to 1991**, which is around forty-six years.

574. During this time, many new technologies were invented or improved. **Computers became more powerful**, allowing officials to access information more quickly. **Televisions became more popular** and allowed people to see news events happening far away as if they were right there themselves!

575. Throughout **the Cold war**, American scientists made many breakthroughs, such as launching communication **satellites like Telstar 1 in July 1962.**

576. **During the Cold War, the US and the Soviet Union competed** to show who was more powerful by developing new technologies like missiles and rockets faster than the other.

577. **This competition led to space exploration,** with both countries launching rockets into space

578. **In 1957, the Soviet Union launched Sputnik 1**, the first artificial satellite ever put into orbit around Earth. It made beeping noises on its way up that people in the US could hear on the radio.

579. **This shocked the Americans** because they had fallen behind the communists. So, in 1958, President Dwight D. Eisenhower **created NASA** (the National Aeronautics and Space Administration).

580. **On April 12th, 1961, Russia sent Yuri Gagarin into space.** He was the first human to reach space, doing so aboard Vostok 1.

581. **A few weeks later, on May 5th, 1961, America sent Alan Shepard** as the first American into space aboard Freedom 7.

582. **Although many accomplishments happened during the Space Race,** it is important to be reminded that what these people were doing was very dangerous. In 1967, American astronauts Gus Grissom, Roger Chaffee, and Ed White died during a pre-launch test when a fire broke out.

583. In 1969, American **Neil Armstrong** became the first person to walk on the moon when he stepped out of Apollo 11. This was a massive milestone for US space exploration and officially ended the Space Race.

584. Although **the Space Race ended in 1969**, there are a few other important achievements to talk about in regard to US space exploration. In 1975, the US sent a probe called **Voyager 1** into space to study the outer solar system and discover the outer limits of the sun's magnetic field.

585. In 1983, **Sally Ride became the first American female astronaut** in space when she went up on the Challenger. This feat shows how far women had come since WWII ended!

586. Also, in 1984, **President Ronald Reagan** proposed his Strategic Defense Initiative (SDI), also known as "Star Wars," which called for building an impenetrable force field around Earth using lasers, satellites, and other weapons! The plan was a bit too complicated for technology at the time and was scrapped in 1993.

587. **After WWII, Germany was split between the democratic West and communist Russia.** The Berlin Wall was built in 1961 by East Germany to separate its people from West Germany. In 1987, President Reagan gave his famous speech, uttering, "Mr. Gorbachev, tear down this wall!" The Berlin Wall would be dismantled about two years later.

588. **The Cold War led to an arms race** (a competition between countries to build bigger and better weapons) between the US and the Soviet Union. Each wanted to protect its people from an attack by the enemy.

589. Although there was an arms race, **the US and the Soviet Union** would not directly war against each other.

590. Instead, they fought in **proxy wars (a war where major powers use another country to fight the war for them)**. One proxy war was the Korean War. It is seen as the first proxy war between democratic and communist powers. **The Korean War** was fought from 1950 to 1953. The war resulted in the division of Korea.

591. **Another proxy war was the Vietnam War**, which took place between 1955 and 1975. The fighting was brutal, and many died. Vietnam was ultimately reunited under a communist regime.

592. **The Cuban Missile Crisis** is one of the most famous events from the Cold War. It was a thirteen-day standoff where Cuba allowed USSR missiles on its soil. The US threatened military action if the missiles stayed there. The crisis brought the Cold War to America's doorstep. Luckily, war was averted.

593. **For years during the Cold War,** the US government created hideouts in case of a nuclear attack, stockpiling food and supplies that could last for months!

594. **The Soviet Union** had a similar plan. Its government built secret cities, some underground, that were designed to hold millions if something ever happened between US and Russia.

595. **During the Cold War, both sides used propaganda** (information meant to influence people's opinion) to spread fear and mistrust among citizens living within their borders.

596. Beginning in the late 1940s, **Senator Joseph McCarthy** went on a witch hunt to find communists and socialists in the United States. Many false accusations were flung, and notable people were targeted. Some famous people who were victims of McCarthyism include **Helen Keller, Charlie Chaplin**, **Leonard Bernstein, Orson Welles, and Lucille Ball.**

597. There was also an intense **rivalry in the Olympic Games** between American athletes and Russians during this time. In **1980, the Olympics was held in Moscow.** America and sixty-four other nations refused to participate.

598. In 1969 and 1979, **the US and Russia signed treaties called SALT I and II** (Strategic Arms Limitation Talks). The treaty limited the number of nuclear weapons each country could have.

599. Although relations could be tense one moment and better the next, the Cold War thawed under the leadership of **Mikhail Gorbachev.** The Cold War ended in 1991 when **the Soviet Union collapsed.** This shift in the international order enabled increased cooperation between the two countries, leading to the International Space Station in 1998. **The end of the Cold War** also opened the door for the sharing of resources and new technologies.

600. **After the Cold War ended in 1991,**

America became the only superpower in the world. It had achieved great success in space exploration and experienced many technological advancements, proving itself to be a powerful nation compared to the rest of the world's countries.

The Civil Rights Movement

This chapter will explore **the history of the civil rights movement in America.** We'll take a look at thirty interesting facts about how African Americans and other minority groups fought for their right to equal treatment under the law.

Discover inspiring heroes like **Rosa Parks** and **Martin Luther King Jr.** We'll also learn more about organizations like the NAACP and SNCC that helped advance civil rights through peaceful protests and legal action!

601. **The civil rights movement** was a struggle for social justice that began in the 1950s and lasted until the late 1960s.

602. It notably sought to **end racial discrimination** against African Americans. Other minority groups, such as Native Americans and Hispanics, also fought for equal rights.

603. The **NAACP** (National Association for the Advancement of Colored People) was formed in 1909. It is still an active organization today and advocates for civil rights and racial justice through legal action, education, and outreach programs.

604. The **Greensboro Four** staged sit-ins at segregated lunch counters throughout North Carolina.

605. **Sit-ins** were an integral part of **the civil rights movement,** as they helped desegregate public spaces like restaurants and movie theaters with peaceful protests. Tens of thousands of people participated in sit-ins during this era.

606. In April 1960, **the Student Nonviolent Coordinating Committee** (SNCC) was formed. It began organizing sit-ins at segregated lunch counters throughout the South in the 1960s.

607. **The Freedom Riders** were groups of people who rode buses across the South in 1961. They challenged the Jim Crow laws. These riders even faced death threats and violence as they protested for equal rights!

608. **The Jim Crow laws** began in the late 19th century and were predominant in the South. These laws discriminated against African Americans. For instance, African American children had to attend a separate school from white children. African Americans had separate drinking fountains and lived in different neighborhoods than whites.

609. In 1896, in **Plessy v. Ferguson,** the US Supreme Court ruled that the Jim Crow laws did not go against the Constitution as long as things were "separate but equal."

610. This law was mostly overruled by the decision of **Brown v. Board of Education.** In 1954, the Supreme Court ruled that racial segregation in public schools went against the Constitution.

611. In 1957, nine African American students, known as the Little Rock Nine, attempted to integrate **Little Rock Central High School in Arkansas.** They received death threats and physical abuse. The National Guard refused to let the students enter until President Eisenhower got involved.

612. **Six-year-old Ruby Bridges** became a symbol of courage when she became African American student at William Frantz Elementary School in New Orleans, Louisiana, in 1960. Despite facing extreme racism, she stayed strong throughout her journey to fight for equality education system United States.

613. **The Black Panther Party** was founded by Huey Newton and Bobby Seale in Oakland, California, in 1966. Members of this group sought to protect African Americans from police brutality through grassroots organization and self-defense tactics, such as armed patrols of neighborhoods.

614. Almost every Black Panther believed that **the Black Power movement** could make a difference in how African Americans were treated. Instead of depending on the government to make changes, the Black Power movement believed blacks should be self-sufficient, which included taking justice into their own hands.

615. **Malcolm X** was a huge proponent of the Black Power movement. He championed social justice through his radical ideology and unapologetic speeches that aimed to empower African Americans and other people of color.

616. **Martin Luther King Jr.** was an activist who sought a more peaceful resolution. While he wasn't part of the Black Power movement, he understood their pain and frustration. King notably gave his iconic **"I Have a Dream"** speech at the March on Washington in 1963, which called for equality among all races and people worldwide.

617. **Rosa Parks is known for refusing to give up her seat on a bus to a white person,** sparking the Montgomery bus boycott, which lasted for more than one year.

618. In 1962, Cesar Chavez formed the **United Farm Workers of America,** a labor union, to fight against unfair wages and working conditions faced by farm workers, specifically those of Hispanic descent living in California. Chavez was part of the Chicano movement, which was similar to the Black Power movement in regard to ideas of nationalism and community empowerment.

619. **The Birmingham church bombing** in 1963 was a turning point for the civil rights movement. Four African American girls died, sparking nationwide outrage and finally pushing President Lyndon B. Johnson to sign the Civil Rights Act of 1964 into law.

620. **The 1964 Civil Rights Act** outlawed segregation nationwide by prohibiting discrimination based on race or color in public places like schools, parks, and businesses.

621. **The Freedom Summer of 1964** saw thousands of activists from all walks of life travel to Mississippi to register African American voters. In 1962, a little over 5 percent of blacks were registered to vote. The Freedom of Summer project was ultimately unsuccessful in its goal, but it did raise attention to the issue blacks faced at the polls.

622. **In February 1965, Malcolm X was assassinated.** He had renounced the Nation of Islam, a US group that is different from traditional Islam, and formed a new group for Muslims. The Nation of Islam was not happy about this, and three members of the group shot him during an assembly. People still wonder if the government was somehow involved in his death.

623. **The 1965 Selma to Montgomery march** was a historical event demonstrating the power of peaceful protest. It ultimately led to Congress passing the Voting Rights Act, which prohibited discrimination when people voted.

624. In August 1965, Congress passed the Voting Rights Act. **African Americans could finally vote** without facing unfair obstacles like literacy tests or poll taxes. The Voting Rights Act was a landmark piece of legislation that outlawed discrimination based on race or color when voting.

625. **On April 4th, 1968, Martin Luther King Jr. was assassinated.** His death spurred nationwide mourning and outrage. His message inspired many to keep fighting for civil rights until justice had been achieved.

626. **In 1968, Congress passed the Fair Housing Act**, which outlawed discrimination based on race or ethnicity when renting, selling, or financing housing across America.

627. In 1969, the Stonewall riots marked the beginning of **the LGBTQ movement.** The riots were sparked when police raided a popular gay bar in New York City. LGBTQ activists united to protest against discrimination and fight for equal rights for all, regardless of sexual orientation.

628. **In 1969, hundreds of Native American activists and supporters occupied Alcatraz Island** for nineteen months. They wanted the island to be returned to them since it had once belonged to the Lakota. Alcatraz had been home to a notorious prison, but it closed in 1964. The protest was not successful, but it did set a precedent for Native American activism.

629. **The 1971 Supreme Court case Swann v Charlotte-Mecklenburg Board of Education** ruled against racial segregation on buses. The Supreme Court ruled that busing students of different races together across district lines promoted integration.

630. **The election of Barack Obama** as the forty-fourth president of the United States showed how far the US had come since the civil rights movement. As the first African American president, Obama's election was a major step forward in terms of racial equality in the nation.

The Gulf War and the War on Terror

This chapter will explore **the history of the Gulf War and the War on Terror,** two significant conflicts that are still impacting the world today. We'll look at some key events, such as Iraq's invasion of **Kuwait** in 1990 and **Operation Desert Storm**.

Additionally, we'll cover other related topics like **drone strikes** and **human rights** violations caused during military interventions.

631. **The Gulf War** was a conflict between Iraq and an international coalition led by the United States that lasted from 1990 to 1991.

632. It began when **Iraq invaded Kuwait** on August 2nd, 1990, and ended with the liberation of Kuwait on February 28th, 1991.

633. **Saddam Hussein** ordered Iraq's invasion of Kuwait. He wanted control over its oilfields and ports for trade purposes and to expand Iraq's power.

634. **Iraq had a powerful military.** Its soldiers took over Kuwait in just two days!

635. **Operation Desert Storm** was the US-led military intervention to liberate Kuwait from Iraqi occupation during the Gulf War in early 1991.

636. Almost a **million soldiers** from the coalition fought in the Gulf War. Most of them were from America. Iraq sent over 650,000 soldiers.

637. After forty-two days of relentless bombing campaigns, **President George H. W. Bush** ordered a ceasefire to be drawn up since most of the Iraqis had surrendered or were killed by that point.

638. **The UN Security Council** declared that Iraq must pay for the damages caused during the war and give up all weapons of mass destruction (WMDs). Iraq eventually agreed. Its military power was greatly reduced.

639. **The war resulted in high casualties among civilians** and the destruction of infrastructure in Iraq and Kuwait. Estimated deaths for civilians range as high as 100,000. Millions of people had to move because of the fighting. A little **over two hundred American soldiers** died in the war.

640. Americans saw **live broadcast news** from the front lines for the first time during the Gulf War.

641. **The War on Terror** is a term used to refer to the global military campaign against terrorist organizations and individuals, especially **Osama bin Laden** and his al-Qaeda network.

642. The War on Terror began shortly after **the September 11th attacks in 2001.** The attacks took nearly three thousand lives.

643. Four planes were hijacked. **Two were flown into the World Trade Center in New York City. One hit the Pentagon.** And another was taken over by the passengers and crashed down in Pennsylvania. It was likely headed to the Capitol.

644. In October 2001, **NATO** invoked its collective defense clause for the first time due to 9/11. This clause states that a NATO country being attacked should be treated as if all the NATO countries are being attacked.

645. The War on Terror has resulted in numerous military interventions **in Afghanistan, Iraq, Pakistan, and Somalia.** For the most part, these interventions have been led by the US.

646. **US forces have conducted air strikes** targeting militant groups in these and other regions in the Middle East.

647. **Several successful missions** have been carried out by international coalition forces. The forces aid local governments in countering terrorist activities.

648. **In 2003, US forces entered Iraq** in search of WMDs and to bring democracy to the people of Iraq. To this day, no major stores of WMDs have ever been found in Iraq.

649. **Saddam Hussein** was overthrown and killed in 2006, ending his reign of terror.

650. In 2011, **Osama bin Laden** was killed after being found hiding in Abbottabad, Pakistan, by US Navy Seals during a raid operation. Osama bin Laden orchestrated 9/11 and was the leader of the terrorist organization called al-Qaeda.

651. Every day, thousands of soldiers face dangers posed by **improvised explosive devices** (IEDs) and **suicide bombers.**

652. The use of **unmanned drones to target terrorists** has been highly debated due to civilian casualties resulting from this practice. It is estimated that in Pakistan alone, drone strikes killed over two thousand civilians between 2004 and 2014.

653. The wars associated with this conflict have received **widespread criticism over human rights** violations and civilian casualties. Both sides are guilty of committing war crimes.

654. In 2014, **NATO declared the war in Afghanistan to be over.** Many US troops stayed in the country. In 2021, the American soldiers left. The Taliban took over the Afghan government.

655. **The War on Terror** has resulted in almost **one million deaths** and tens of millions of displaced people. So far, the US has spent an estimated eight trillion dollars to fight terrorism.

656. It is believed that countries with strong **US military presence** have significantly decreased terrorism-related activities since 2001.

657. This conflict significantly **impacted international relations** between different nations, especially those directly involved or affected by it.

658. Since 2001, **the War on Terror** has caused governments to put stricter surveillance laws in place, which has led to restrictions on civil liberties in many countries.

659. **US Special Forces** continue operations in Iraq, providing training and support to local security personnel tasked with countering terrorist threats.

660. After a two-decade-long conflict between coalition forces and terrorist factions, such as al-**Qaeda and ISIS**, there are still active conflicts occurring in many regions worldwide. There is currently **no precise end date set for this war.** Many believe it is unlikely terrorism will ever end.

The United States of America in the 21st Century

This chapter will explore the many important events that have taken place **in the United States in the 21st century.** With these thirty facts, you'll gain insight into how this nation has developed over a major world power. We'll discover their advances in technology, global relationships, health care reform, and more. Discover why understanding this country's **recent history is so critical to understanding its future!**

661. **In 2003, the United States invaded Iraq** and overthrew Saddam Hussein in a little over a month.

662. **The United States has been involved in multiple international conflicts** in the 21st century in places like Syria and Libya as part of its efforts toward global stability and peace.

663. **After Hurricane Katrina** struck New Orleans in 2005, President George W. Bush signed off on $10.5 billion worth of relief aid for victims affected by this disaster.

664. In 2005, Americans were hit by three major hurricanes within weeks: **Katrina** (August), **Rita** (September), and **Wilma** (October).

665. **The US elected** its first African American president, **Barack Obama**, in 2008.

666. In 2009, the **US government passed an economic stimulus package** to help revive the economy from a financial crisis that had caused massive unemployment rates across America and serious stock market declines

667. In 2009, **President Obama won his Nobel Peace Prize** for promoting nuclear disarmament while leading negotiations with foreign leaders on international issues of major importance.

668. **The Obama administration passed a vital health care reform** bill commonly known as "Obamacare" in 2010, which increased access to medical coverage across America.

669. In 2010, US scientists created the world's first synthetic organism from DNA strands in a laboratory.

670. The **"Occupy Wall Street"** movement was a protest against corporate greed and economic inequality. It spread quickly throughout cities across America, including New York City, where it began.

671. **The NASA rover Curiosity landed on Mars** for exploration in 2012. The project cost an estimated 2.5 billion dollars, making it one of the most expensive space missions ever undertaken.

672. In 2013, **Edward Snowden** leaked government documents revealing information on US surveillance programs against citizens and foreign countries.

673. **Marriage equality was finally approved nationwide** after legal battles that lasted nearly ten years. The Supreme Court ruled on the Obergefell v. Hodges case, declaring that same-sex marriage was a constitutional right in June 2015.

674. **After several years** of negotiations between various parties, Iran reached a nuclear agreement with world powers, including America, in 2015. **Iran agreed to reduce its stockpile of uranium.**

675. On August 21st, 2017, **a total solar eclipse crossed fourteen states**, providing millions with a unique view of this natural phenomenon.

676. **The US has seen significant advances in technology** during this century, from smartphones to self-driving cars. Artificial intelligence (AI) applications are being developed all over the country.

677. **Apple Inc. was founded by Steve Jobs** and others in 1976. In 2010, it was worth over $65 billion. Two years later, it was worth $156 billion.

678. **Social media networks,** such as **Twitter** and **Facebook,** have become ubiquitous worldwide since they were launched at the start of the 21st century. These platforms allow billions to connect instantly across continents without barriers.

679. **In 2014, Google purchased Nest Labs**, making it one of the first large companies to invest heavily in home automation techs like smart thermostats, security systems, and other devices.

680. As of 2022, **the US is home to the world's largest economy,** accounting for over 15 percent of the global GDP (gross domestic product).

681. In 2019, almost **165.5 million people visited the United States,** making it one of the most popular tourist destinations in the world.

682. **America's per capita GDP is one of the highest in the world.** It is estimated at around $65,000 in 2020, making it an attractive destination for those seeking economic opportunities abroad.

683. **The US has seen a surge in mass shootings** across the nation since 2007, leading to numerous debates and discussions on gun law legislation.

684. **The US is a major contributor to greenhouse gas emissions.** As part of the Paris Climate Agreement, the US committed to reducing its emissions by 26 to 28 percent from 2005 levels by 2025. Although the US planned to leave the Hillary Paris Agreement, Biden recommitted to the agreement when he became president.

685. In 2016, **America elected its first female candidate for president, Clinton,** although she ultimately lost to Donald Trump.

686. In 2020, **NASA launched the Perseverance rover,** which landed on Mars in 2021. As of this writing, it is successfully collecting data from the red planet to help study its environment.

687. In 2020, **the United States experienced** an unusually high number of cases and deaths due to **a virus outbreak.** In response to this pandemic, the United States took action in 2021 to provide relief for citizens in terms of health and economic stability.

688. As of 2022, **the US had distributed 613 million doses**. The country also enacted the American Rescue Plan in 2021, a $1.9 trillion economic stimulus package. The government also passed additional initiatives aimed at providing relief during these difficult times.

689. On January 6th, 2021, **pro-Trump supporters stormed Capitol Hill to protest** and stop the certification of Joe Biden's win against Trump. As of this writing, investigations are being made into whether President Trump encouraged them.

690. In 2022, **the US continued addressing major challenges** such as climate change while working toward restoring international relations through investments in renewable energy sources and cyber security projects, among others.

Section 2: Uncovering More Fascinating Facts of American History

Major Political Events That Shaped Modern-day Politics

This chapter will delve into **the major political events of the world and the US**. These thirty facts will explore key moments in history, such as **the American Revolution, the Civil War,** and more recent occurrences like the **MeToo movement.** We'll also look at how these events impacted US foreign policy, civil rights movements, and economic power. By understanding these pivotal moments in time, we gain a greater appreciation for their role in shaping the current political landscape.

691. **The Magna Carta** of 1215 was an important document in English history that limited the power of the king and established fundamental rights for all people, including nobles. **The Magna Carta** greatly influenced the US Constitution.

692. **In 1776, America declared independence from Britain** and became a new nation with its own laws and government system

693. **The US Constitution was written in 1787** and is the supreme law of the United States. It is the oldest written constitution still in use today and outlines the structure of the federal government.

694. **The French Revolution began in 1789,** with people seeking to overthrow the monarchy and establish a democratic republic instead. Other revolutions followed, many of which were inspired by the American and French Revolutions.

695. **The Louisiana Purchase** was a significant land transaction in 1803. The United States paid France $15 million for 828,000 square miles west of the Mississippi River. This purchase more than doubled the size of the United States and opened up the country's westward expansion.

696. **The War of 1812** was fought to gain control of the Great Lakes and the Canadian border. The conflict resulted in a stalemate. However, it established the US as a powerful nation, as the country was able to show its strength to the rest of the world.

697. **The Mexican-American War** lasted from 1846 to 1848. The war resulted in the US gaining more than 500,000 square miles of land, including parts of modern-day California, Arizona, New Mexico, and Nevada, among others.

698. **The Communist Manifesto** was written by Karl Marx and Friedrich Engels in 1848. The text argued for a classless society based on common ownership of production forces, eventually leading to uprisings across Europe in the 19th century.

699. **During the Industrial Revolution** (1760–1850), machines replaced manual labor around the world, leading to increased economic growth and poverty among certain groups of workers.

700. **Slavery was abolished in many countries** in the 19th century, as people began to increasingly view it as morally wrong.

701. **The Civil War** was fought **between the Northern and Southern states** of the United States from 1861 to 1865. The war was fought over the issue of slavery, and it resulted in the abolition of slavery and the reunification of the United States.

702. **The Berlin Conference** of 1884/85 saw European nations carve up Africa for their interests, leading to a long period of colonization and exploitation by foreign powers on the continent. Although the US did not colonize Africa, it did play a role on the continent with the formation of Liberia.

703. **The Spanish-American War** was fought over Cuban independence in 1898. It resulted in the US gaining control of several Spanish territories, including Puerto Rico and the Philippines.

704. **World War I** (1914–1918) was fought between the Central powers (Germany, Austria-Hungary, Turkey, and Bulgaria) and the Allied forces (Britain, France, Russia, and the US). It resulted in millions of deaths and changed many borders, creating the map we are familiar with today.

705. **The Great Depression** was a severe economic recession that began in 1929 and lasted until the early 1940s. The Great Depression had a devastating effect on the world's economy and resulted in widespread unemployment and poverty.

706. In 1963, **President John F. Kennedy was assassinated.** The news shocked the US. Three other notable people would be assassinated in the 1960s: Malcolm X, Martin Luther King Jr., and Bobby Kennedy (JFK's brother), who was running for president.

707. **The Vietnam War** was a conflict between North and South Vietnam. It lasted from 1955 to 1975. The US became involved in the war in 1965, and its involvement was highly controversial. The war had a lasting impact on the US economy, politics, and foreign policy.

708. **The Watergate scandal** was a political scandal in the 1970s. A group of men broke into the Democratic National Committee headquarters at the Watergate Hotel and Office building in Washington, DC. The scandal resulted in Republican **President Richard Nixon's resignation** and impacted US politics for decades to come.

709. **The Iranian hostage crisis** was a diplomatic crisis that lasted from 1979 to 1981. Iranian militants took over the US Embassy in Tehran, holding fifty-two diplomats and civilians hostage for 444 days. When Iraq invaded Iran in 1980, Iran reached out to the US for help. The hostages would all be released by 1981, although the militants began releasing groups of hostages in 1979.

710. **Reaganomics is the term used to refer to President Ronald Reagan's** economic policies. He implemented several conservative policies, including tax cuts, deregulation, and a firm anti-communist foreign policy. Reaganomics had a lasting impact on US politics and economics.

711. **The Iraq War** was a conflict between the United States and Iraq that lasted from 2003 to 2011. The war was fought over Iraq's weapons of mass destruction and Saddam Hussein's brutal regime. The war resulted in the overthrow of Saddam Hussein and the establishment of a democratic government in Iraq.

712. **The Arab Spring** was a series of protests and uprisings in the Middle East and North Africa that occurred between 2010 and 2012. The protests resulted in the overthrow of several dictatorships and had a profound impact on US foreign policy in the region.

713. The 2012 **was between incumbent President Barack Obama and Republican challenger Mitt Romney.** The election was highly contested, but President Obama was reelected, making him the first African American president to serve two terms in office.

714. **In 2015, the US Supreme Court's decision on same-sex marriage was a landmark victory for LGBTQ** rights and served as a stepping stone for further progress in the area of civil rights.

715. **The 2016 presidential election was between Democratic nominee Hillary Clinton and Republican nominee Donald Trump**. The latter was elected president, making him the first president in US history to be elected without prior political or military experience.

716. **The 2016 presidential election was notable for the role of social media**. Both campaigns used social media platforms, such as **Twitter and Facebook**, extensively, and the election has been described as the "first social media election" in US history.

717. **The MeToo movement is an international movement that seeks to end sexual violence and harassment.** The movement began in 2006 but picked up momentum in 2017. MeToo has brought awareness to the everyday issues girls and women face.

718. **The 2017 Tax Cuts and Jobs Act was a sweeping tax reform package** passed by Congress and signed into law by President Trump in December 2017. The package was highly controversial, but it significantly impacted the US economy and led to a large reduction in taxes for many Americans.

719. **In 2018, the US became the world's largest producer of crude oil** and kept its position until 2021, revolutionizing the global energy market and increasing America's financial and political clout on the world stage.

720. **The 2020 presidential election was between incumbent President Donald Trump and Democratic challenger Joe Biden.** The election was highly contested, but Joe Biden was elected president, making him the oldest person to be elected president in US history.

Sports Achievements during US History

This chapter will explore some of **the incredible sports achievements made by US athletes throughout history.** We'll take a look at thirty facts to gain insight into how **Americans have dominated Olympic and World Cup competitions** and broken records in baseball, basketball, and boxing.

Learn **why US teams continue to be so successful today** due to their commitment to excellence through dedication and hard work!

721. **The United States** has been one of the most successful countries in the modern Olympic Games. As of this writing, it has won over one thousand gold medals!

722. **Women's sports** have made a major impact on US history. Babe Didrikson Zaharias became one of the greatest American female athletes, winning two gold medals in track and field. Wilma Rudolph also found success in the same category in the 1960 Rome Olympics, winning three gold medals.

723. **Bob Beamon broke his long jump world record** and current Olympic mark with a leap of 8.90 meters (29 feet, 2.5 inches) at the Mexico City Olympics in 1968, setting a record that wouldn't be broken until 1991!

724. **Dan Gable** is considered one of **wrestling's best athletes** after **winning the 1972 Summer Olympics** without giving up a single point. He pinned every one of his opponents and scored a gold medal, the first American wrestler to do so in twelve years.

725. In 1980, a hockey game called the **"Miracle on Ice"** took place. It was one of the biggest upsets in sporting history. **The US men's hockey team, composed mostly of amateurs, beat the Soviets,** who were heavy favorites for that year's Olympics Games! The "Miracle on Ice" became an iconic underdog story.

726. **The 1984 Los Angeles Olympics was sensational for the US.** American athletes won 174 medals, including 83 gold, 61 silver, and 30 bronze medals, making it one of America's most successful Olympic performances.

727. **Tonya Harding** made history by becoming the first American female figure skater to land a triple axel jump in the 1991 US Figure Skating championships competition. Her accomplishments on the ice tend to be overshadowed by her controversies off the ice.

728. In 1992, the **US Dream Team was created.** This team consisted of active NBA (National Basketball Associate) players. Some of the members included **Larry Bird, Michael Jordan, Magic Johnson, Charles Barkley, Patrick Ewing, and Scottie Pippen.** It has been called the greatest sports team ever assembled.

729. In 1996, **Michael Johnson** became an iconic athlete for his performance in the Atlanta Olympics when he won the 200m and 400m races. He is the only male athlete so far who has been able to do so in the same Olympics.

730. **The Boston Marathon** is an annual marathon that started on April 19th, 1897. It is traditionally held on Patriot's Day, which commemorates Paul Revere's ride.

731. **Jack Johnson** became America's very first African American world heavyweight boxing champion in 1908.

732. **Joe Louis** became a world heavyweight **boxing champion for twelve years,** from 1937 to 1949, becoming an iconic figure for African Americans. He defended his title twenty-five times!

733. **The first professional football game** was played in 1892. The Allegheny Athletic Association was pitted against the Pittsburgh Athletic Club.

734. **The American Professional Football Association** was formed in 1920. Two years later, it changed its name to the National Football League (NFL). Football is considered to be the most-watched sport in the US.

735. **The Super Bowl** is the final playoff game between the best of the best in football. It is one of the most-watched TV programs in American history and is

736. **The New York Yankees baseball team** is one of the most successful sports teams in the US. The team has won twenty-seven World Series championships. Some of the most iconic players in the history of baseball played for the Yankees, including **Babe Ruth**, **Joe DiMaggio**, **Mickey Mantle**, and **Lou Gehring**.

737. **Willie Mays** is considered one of the greatest baseball players, with 660 career home runs, a 1954 Most Valuable Player Award, and 23 All-Star selections throughout his 22-year-long career!

738. **Baseball legend Hank Aaron** hit 755 home runs over 21 seasons, which set the record then. He is known as the "Home Run King" of Major League Baseball (MLB).

739. In 2004, **the Boston Red Sox** ended an eighty-six-year-long drought when they finally won their first World Series title since 1918 by sweeping the St. Louis Cardinals in four games, giving fans reason to celebrate after so many years of misery.

740. **Basketball was invented** by James Naismith in Springfield, Massachusetts, in 1891 and is now a popular sport around the world.

741. In 1996, **the Chicago Bulls** won seventy-two of eighty-two games during the regular season, setting the NBA record for most wins in a single year! The Golden State Warriors upset that record in their 2015/16 season, winning seventy-three games in a single season.

742. **Michael Jordan played for the Chicago Bulls** and is one of the most celebrated US athletes today. He has many accomplishments, two of which are winning the NBA championship six times and being the NBA MVP five times.

743. **The US Women's National Basketball Association** has been incredibly successful since its formation in 1996. As of this writing, the US Women's National Team has one of the best records in the Olympics, suffering no losses since 1992. It is also first in the FIBA rankings.

744. **Women's team sports** have grown significantly in US history, especially after Title IX legislation passed in 1972 that allowed female athletes access to equal educational opportunities and funding in sports.

745. **The US Women's National Soccer Team** (USWNT) has been incredibly successful since its formation in 1985, winning four Olympic gold medals from 1996 to 2012. It has also won four Women's World Cups in 1991, 1999, 2015, and 2019.

746. **Billie Jean King** became one of the most iconic female tennis players after she won a legendary match against Bobby Riggs at the Houston Astrodome in 1973, known as the "Battle of the Sexes."

747. **Venus and Serena Williams** both made history by becoming the two highest-ranked female tennis players in 2002. The sisters have achieved amazing things on the court. Venus Williams has won four Olympic gold medals, seven Grand Slams, and five Wimbledon championships. Serena Williams also holds four Olympic gold medals and thirty-nine Grand Slams. The sisters set an example for young women all over the world.

748. Although **hockey (the NHL)** is not as popular as football or basketball, it is still one of the major sports franchises in the US. In the 1995/96 season, **the Detroit Red Wings had** the most wins in a single season. The Tampa Bay Lightning tied the Wings' sixty-two wins in the 2018/19 season.

749. **Tiger Woods** set several records during his historic win at the 1997 Masters Tournament by becoming not only the youngest winner but also the first person African American golfer to do so. In 2001, he became the youngest player to complete a Grand Slam (winning all top four major professional golf tournaments in a career).

750. **Lance Armstrong** made history by becoming the only person to win seven consecutive Tour de France titles between 1999 to 2005 before being stripped of all his wins due to doping allegations in 2012.

Military Conflicts Fought by Americans

This chapter will explore **the various military conflicts fought by Americans** throughout history. We'll take a look at thirty facts about conflicts, from the **Revolutionary War** to the ongoing **war in Syria.**

751. **The American Revolutionary War** was fought between Britain and the American colonies from 1775 to 1783. The war was fought after the American colonies declared their independence from Britain and sought to establish a new nation.

752. The war saw a variety of battles fought between the two sides, with the British eventually being defeated by the American forces **at the Battle of Yorktown in 1781**. The war ended with the signing of the Treaty of Paris in 1783, which officially recognized the United States of America as an independent nation.

753. **The Barbary Wars** were a series of conflicts fought between the United States and the Barbary states in North Africa from 1801 to 1815.

754. The wars were fought after **the Barbary states began to attack American merchant ships** in the Mediterranean and demand tribute from the United States. The United States eventually gained control of the region. The First Barbary War ended with the signing of the Treaty of Tripoli in 1805. The Second Barbary War lasted for only three days and also ended in an American victory.

755. **The War of 1812** was a conflict fought between Britain and the United States from 1812 to 1815. The war was triggered by various disputes between the two countries, including American anger over British interference with American shipping and the impressment of American sailors into the British navy.

756. **The British were eventually defeated in the War of 1812**. One of the Americans' greatest victories was the Battle of New Orleans, which happened after the war ended. The conflict officially ended with the signing of the Treaty of Ghent in 1815.

757. **The American Indian Wars** were a series of conflicts fought between Native American tribes and the United States government from the early 17th century to the early 20th century.

758. The wars were fought mainly to gain control of Native American tribal lands and to **push Native Americans from their ancestral homelands.** Many different tribes were involved in the conflicts, but the US eventually gained control of much of the western part of the continent.

759. **The Seminole Wars** were a series of conflicts fought between the United States and the Seminole tribe from 1816 to 1858. The wars were fought after the Seminoles refused to leave their tribal lands in Florida, which the United States wanted to use to expand its territory. The United States eventually gained control of the region.

760. **The Mexican-American War** was fought between the United States and Mexico from 1846 to 1848.

761. The war was triggered by a dispute over the border between the two countries. The United States eventually claimed victory and gained control of much of what is today the southwestern United States. The war ended with the signing of the **Treaty of Guadalupe Hidalgo in 1848.**

762. **The American Civil War** was fought between the Union and the Confederate States of America from 1861 to 1865.

763. **The war was fought after the Confederate States seceded from the Union to establish a new nation.** The war was bloody, with both sides suffering many casualties. The war ended with the surrender of the Confederate Army at Appomattox Court House in 1865.

764. **The Spanish-American War** was fought between Spain and the United States in 1898. The war was triggered by the sinking of the USS Maine in Havana Harbor, Cuba, in February 1898.

765. **The United States claimed victory in the war** and gained control of islands in the Caribbean and Pacific. The war ended with the Treaty of Paris in 1898.

766. **The Philippine-American War** was a conflict fought between the United States and Filipino revolutionaries from 1899 to 1902.

767. **The Filipino revolutionaries'** desire for independence from US control triggered the war. American soldiers were ultimately able to occupy the islands and put down the revolutionaries for the most part.

768. **World War I** was fought between the Allied and Central powers **from 1914 to 1918**. The war was triggered by the assassination of Archduke Franz Ferdinand of Austria-Hungary in June 1914, with the Allied powers eventually claiming victory and gaining control of much of Europe. World War I changed how conflicts were fought and ended with the signing of the Treaty of Versailles in 1919.

769. **World War II** was fought between the Allied and Axis powers **from 1939 to 1945**. The war was triggered by the invasion of Poland by Nazi Germany in September 1939, although the Allied powers eventually claimed victory. The war ended with the surrender of Japan in 1945.

770. **The Korean War** was a conflict fought between North Korea and South Korea from **1950 to 1953**. The war was triggered by North Korea's invasion of South Korea in June 1950.

771. Although North Korea made some gains, Korea did not become united. After the war, Korea remained divided. An armistice agreement was signed, so the war technically never ended.

772. **The Vietnam War** was fought between North Vietnam and South Vietnam from **1955 to 1975.** The war was triggered by the North Vietnamese invasion of South Vietnam in 1955.

773. Other nations entered the Vietnam War, with the United States sending hundreds of thousands of troops to the area. **The Paris Peace Accords was signed in 1973,** and two years later, North Vietnam took over South Vietnam.

774. **The Gulf War** was fought between Iraq and a coalition of forces, including the United States, from 1990 to 1991.

775. **The Iraqi invasion of Kuwait** triggered the First Gulf War in August 1990, with the coalition forces eventually claiming victory and gaining control of the region. The war ended with a ceasefire agreement in 1991.

776. **The Iraq War** was fought between the United States and Iraq **from 2003 to 2011**. The war was triggered by the US invasion of Iraq in 2003.

777. **The United States won the war** and toppled Saddam Hussein's regime. In 2011, the last US troops left Iraq.

778. **The War in Afghanistan** is a conflict that lasted from 2001 to 2021.

779. The war was triggered by the US invasion of Afghanistan in 2001 **after the Taliban refused to hand over Osama bin Laden.** The United States eventually found Osama bin Laden, but it was not successful in the war, as the Taliban took over the country.

780. **The Syrian Civil War** is a conflict that broke out in 2011 between the Syrian government and various rebel groups. The war was triggered by the Syrian government's crackdown on dissidents. As of this writing, the conflict is still ongoing.

Technology Revolution in the US

This chapter will explore the incredible and groundbreaking technologies that have revolutionized our lives over the past couple of centuries. Through these thirty facts, you'll gain insight into some of **the most significant inventions in history,** such as **telephones, automobiles, and computers!** We'll investigate how these products changed communication and transportation forever. Understanding this fascinating technological revolution is essential for keeping up with a rapidly changing world!

781. **The technological revolution began in the US** in the late 1800s, with new technologies like telephones and cars being developed.

782. **Alexander Graham Bell** is credited with inventing the telephone in 1876. The telephone changed how people communicated.

783. In 1877, **Thomas Edison** invented the phonograph, which could record and play sounds.

784. **Thomas Edison was a prolific American inventor**. He also invented the machine called the Kinetoscope, which could show moving pictures!

785. **The Wright Brothers** are credited with inventing powered human flight after their successful first airplane flight on December 17th, 1903, near Kitty Hawk, North Carolina.

786. **Henry Ford's Model-T car** was released in 1908, revolutionizing transportation around America and making travel easier than ever.

787. **Computers were first introduced into the workplace** in the 1950s and 1960s, making tasks like calculating numbers much faster. Computers really became popular in the 1980s.

788. **German American inventor Ralph Baer** created the first digital video game in 1967 called **"Brown Box,"** which allowed two players to play against each other. The game later morphed into the first console game called Magnavox Odyssey.

789. In 1968, ARPANET **(Advanced Research Projects Agency Network)** sent its first message across computers connected over a network; this is the beginning of what we now know as the internet!

790. **Mobile cell phones** were invented by Martin Cooper in 1973. Cellphones would eventually allow people to make calls on the go without being tied down to landlines or payphones.

791. **Apple released its first personal computer,** the Apple I, in 1976, revolutionizing how people used computers at home and for work.

792. The 1980s saw an explosion of tech products, with companies like **Nintendo** (based in Japan) releasing their iconic gaming console known as NES **(Nintendo Entertainment System).**

793. **IBM introduced the Personal Computer** in 1981, allowing people to use computers for daily tasks and entertainment.

794. In 1994, the popular web browser **Netscape**

Navigator was released, which made surfing the internet much easier!

795. **MP3 players** were introduced in 1997 by a South Korean company, drastically changing how people listened to music. We still like to listen to our choice of music today on the go!

796. **Google** became the most used search engine by 2000, becoming a household name worldwide.

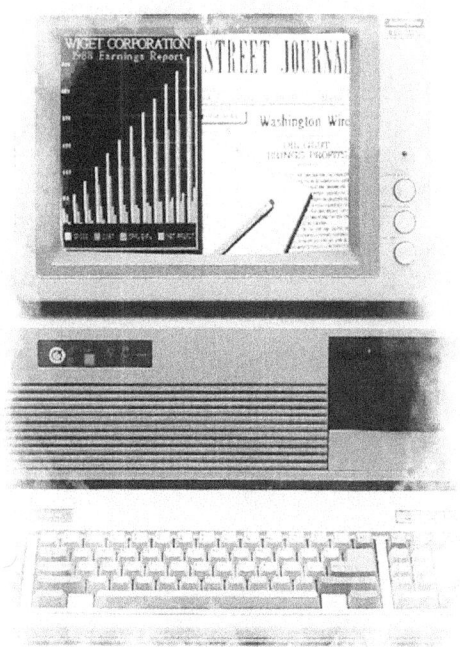

797. **Wi-Fi (Wireless Fidelity)** technology was released to consumers in 1997 but didn't become widely available until 2003, when it started appearing in more and more places, like schools, businesses, and homes.

798. **Social media** sites, such as **Facebook,** began popping up in the late 1990s; now, almost everyone has an account on one or more social media platforms.

799. **The Apple iPhone** was released in 2007, bringing revolutionary touchscreen technology into people's lives and making communication even simpler.

800. **Smartphones** with advanced features emerged shortly after the iPhone, revolutionizing how we interact with each other today.

801. Although apps **(applications)** have been around since the late 1990s, they didn't become really popular until around 2008. Today, we use apps to play games and order food.

802. **3D printing** has been around since the 1980s but recently became much more affordable and accessible. People can use 3D printing to print out almost anything they need!

803. **Wearable technology,** such as fitness trackers, has become popular over the past decade. These devices help us monitor our physical activity and health.

804. **Virtual reality (VR)** headsets have been

around since 1975, but they didn't become readily available to the public until the mid-2010s. VR puts users into digital environments that look and feel like real life.

805. **Artificial intelligence (AI)** is used in many aspects of our lives today, such as self-driving cars and voice assistants.

806. **Augmented reality (AR),** which was first experimented with back in 1994, has grown increasingly popular over recent years. Augmented reality combines real life with the virtual world. Pokémon Go is a great example of an augmented reality app.

807. **Autonomous drones** are now being used for delivery services and surveillance tasks due to their increased accuracy and efficiency.

808. **Quantum computing** is a relatively new field of computer science that's pushing the boundaries of what computers can do based on quantum theory.

809. **Robotic technologies** have significantly advanced in recent years. Robots are now able to complete complex tasks with precision.

810. **Cloud computing** allows people to store their data online to access it from anywhere without worrying about losing it!

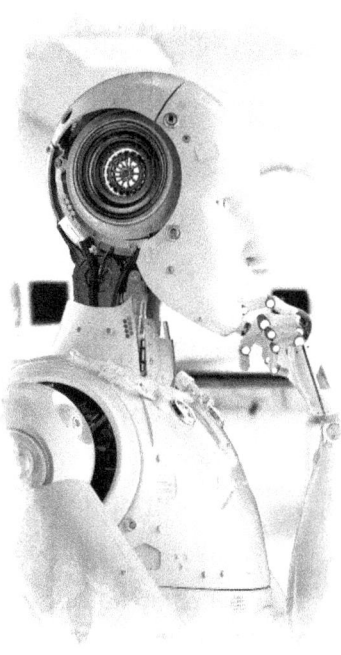

The Women's Rights Movement in America

This chapter will explore the history and progress of **the women's rights movement in America.** We'll look at thirty facts to discover how influential figures such as **Susan B. Anthony, Alice Paul,** and **Gloria Steinem** helped bring about major changes for women throughout US history.

Discover how organizations like NOW **(National Organization for Women)**, social media platforms, and protests are continuing this struggle today.

811. **The women's rights movement in the United States** took a huge step forward in 1848 at Seneca Falls, New York.

812. **The Seneca Falls Convention** was organized by Elizabeth Cady Stanton and Lucretia Mott, who wanted to gain equal rights for all women.

813. In 1869, **Susan B. Anthony and Elizabeth Cady Stanton** created the National Woman Suffrage Association, which pushed for a constitutional amendment to give women the right to vote.

814. **Wyoming** became the first state to grant full voting rights to women in 1890.

815. A major milestone came in 1920 when Congress ratified **the Nineteenth Amendment,** granting suffrage nationwide after decades of activism from both men and women.

816. In 1960, **the first birth control pill** was approved by the FDA, giving women more freedom in their choices regarding pregnancy and sex.

817. Women gained more freedom in the 1960s when they were able to open bank accounts on their own.

818. In 1963, **Betty Friedan released The Feminine Mystique**, which helped bring awareness to the women's rights movement and sparked a resurgence in the fight for equality.

819. President John F. Kennedy signed **the Equal Pay Act** in 1963, which was designed to stop pay discrimination.

820. **After gaining suffrage, many organizations were formed.** One organization was NOW (National Organization for Women), which was founded in 1966.

821. California became the first state to pass **a no-fault divorce law** in 1969. No-fault divorce laws mean that neither party has to provide an instance of wrongdoing. Divorce rates rose as a result.

822. **Gloria Steinem** became one of the founders of Ms. magazine in 1971. The magazine dealt with women's issues and featured feminist articles.

823. In 1972, **Title IX was passed**, which prohibited discrimination against girls and women in educational programs that receive federal funding.

824. **Roe v. Wade** was ruled on in 1973. The Supreme Court decided that women had the right to decide if they wanted an abortion.

825. In 1974, t**he Equal Credit Opportunity Act was passed.** This act made it illegal for creditors to discriminate against applicants based on their sex, race, religion, or marital status.

826. **The Pregnancy Discrimination Act** of 1978 protects pregnant women from being discriminated against in the workplace. The act requires employers to treat pregnant women the same as other employees and not to discriminate against them.

827. **Alice Paul** laid the groundwork for the Equal Rights Amendment (ERA). The amendment was approved by Congress in 1972. However, it failed to gain ratification from enough states for adoption into the Constitution due to strong opposition from conservative groups, such as Phyllis Schlafly's STOP ERA Campaign.

828. Although many women fought for equality, many women didn't want things to change. STOP ("**Stop Taking Our Privileges"**) fought against things like the ERA because they worried it would take away certain privileges like separate restrooms for men and women.

829. In 1981, **Sandra Day O'Connor** became the first woman to sit on the Supreme Court.

830. In 1992, **the US passed the Family and Medical Leave Act** (FMLA), which allows women and men to take up to twelve weeks of unpaid leave per year for certain situations (like taking care of a newborn) without fear of losing their job or health insurance coverage. This was an important milestone in **protecting workers' rights** in the workforce.

831. Another key change came in 1994 when **President Bill Clinton established the Violence Against Women Act.** This office works to end violence against women and girls throughout the United States by supporting victims and holding offenders accountable.

832. **The Lilly Ledbetter Fair Pay Act** was passed in 2009 to strengthen existing equal pay laws. It also allows employees to file discrimination complaints if they have been underpaid due to their gender or race, regardless of how long ago it occurred.

833. In 2012, **the Violence Against Women Act** was passed, which expanded protection for victims of domestic violence and sexual assault. This was a major victory for the women's rights movement in America, as it extended protections to more victims and provided more resources for survivors of abuse.

834. The year 2016 saw the passing of **the Every Student Succeeds Act**, which replaced No Child Left Behind. The act holds schools accountable for the success of all students, regardless of gender, race, or disability.

835. In 2009, **the White House Council on Women and Girls was formed** to advise the president on issues that are important to women and girls throughout America, such as education, economic opportunities, and health care.

836. **The council was disbanded during Trump's presidency,** but President Joe Biden reinstated it, this time calling it the White House Gender Policy Council.

837. **A milestone came in 2020** when Congress passed legislation guaranteeing twelve weeks of paid parental leave to all federal employees, regardless of gender.

838. **The year 2021 saw even further advancements** toward equal pay through legislation introduced at state levels across America to close gender wage gaps within specific industries, such as finance and health care.

839. In 2022, **the US Supreme Court overturned Roe v. Wade.** At the moment, abortion rights reside at the state level. Even conservative states like Kentucky had enough support to defeat state legislation aimed at prohibiting abortion.

840. **Organizations and activists continue to push for changes in women's rights** on a global scale today through protests and social media platforms, such as Twitter and Instagram.

Music, Art, and Literature Movements during American History

This chapter will explore **the fascinating movements in American music, art, and literature** from 1920 to today. We'll examine thirty facts about these trends, including the Harlem Renaissance, the folk music of the Great Depression, jazz, and abstract expressionism. Learn some interesting facts about punk rock and hip-hop. Discover how **artists have used their work to reflect current events** or express opinions on social issues while challenging traditional conventions.

841. **The Harlem Renaissance** in the 1920s was a time of great African American art, music, and literature.

842. **Folk music,** such as blues and country, was popular during the Great Depression.

843. **Abstract expressionism** was a significant art movement that began in New York City during the 1940s and 1950s. Artists focused on expressing emotion through abstract shapes and colors on canvas or paper without using patterns or recognizable images.

844. **Rock and roll** emerged from rhythm and blues (R&B) music in the late 1940s. The popularity of the genre took off thanks to artists like Chuck Berry.

845. **Jazz musicians**, such as **Miles Davis** and **John Coltrane,** created new sounds in the 1950s, departing from the swing band music that was popular decades prior.

846. **The Beatnik movement** was an artistic subculture of writers, poets, and artists who rebelled against conventional society during the late 1950s and early 1960s.

847. **Pop art began in the 1950s and 1960s** as a reaction to abstract expressionism. These artists used recognizable everyday images from pop culture, such as comics, advertisements, and product packaging.

848. **Minimalist art** became popular in the late 1950s and early 1960s. This style of art features simple geometric shapes that are meant to draw attention away from physical forms toward ideas about space or color instead.

849. **The British Invasion happened** in the mid-1960s, bringing Americans famous bands like the Beatles, the Rolling Stones, and the Who, just to name a few.

850. Protest songs became very popular in the 1960s. Many **songwriters spoke out against the Vietnam War.**

851. **The feminist art movement** of the late 1960s sought to create gender equality through artwork by highlighting issues women faced at that time, such as domestic violence and unequal pay for the same work as men.

852. **Postmodern literature** was popular in the 1960s. It uses elements of irony and parody while questioning traditional texts' roles within society.

853. Another popular **type of literature was realism,** which sought to describe reality without embellishments. These texts often involve ordinary people struggling with everyday life problems.

854. **Surrealism literature** uses dreamlike images and symbols to explore complex ideas about life and reality without society's traditional structure or rules.

855. **The black arts movement** lasted from 1965 to 1975. It was an African American literary and artistic movement that sought to create works that addressed themes of racism and oppression.

856. **Punk rock** emerged in the mid-1970s with its driving beats and rebellious lyrics that spoke out against social injustices like racism and poverty.

857. **Punk rockers embraced DIY principles** by encouraging people to make their music instead of relying on major record labels or radio stations for exposure.

858. **Hip-hop was born in New York City** during the 1970s when DJs started mixing samples of different recordings, creating something entirely new in the process.

859. **Postmodern architecture** became popular in the late 1970s. It relies heavily on abstract shapes and curves instead of traditional lines and angles, creating visually stunning buildings!

860. **Poetry slams** became popular in Chicago in the mid-1980s. Poets recite spoken word poetry before crowds and are judged on not only their poems but also their performance.

861. **Grunge music** emerged in Seattle during the mid-1980s. This type of music is known for its loud guitars, distorted sounds, and lyrics about alienation or disaffection from society.

862. **Blues music** enjoyed new popularity in the 1990s, as African American music, literature, and art flourished again after decades of struggle and oppression.

863. **Country music** has been popular since the 1920s but experienced a resurgence in popularity during the 1990s thanks to artists like **Tim McGraw**.

864. **Pop music** has been popular since the mid-1950s and has evolved greatly over the decades.

865. **Latinx writers** have made significant contributions to US literature by writing stories that reflect their culture and experiences living in America.

866. **Many Native American** cultures still practice their traditional arts, including weaving baskets from willow branches or painting images on hides using natural dyes.

867. **Contemporary dance** is a type of performance art that combines different styles, such as modern dance, ballet, and hip-hop.

868. **Street art** is a type of public art that uses graffiti, murals, and stencils to tell stories about current events or express the artist's opinion on social issues.

869. **Street photography** captures everyday moments in public spaces, such as parks, streets, or markets. These photos often depict emotion-filled scenes.

870. **Contemporary art** is an umbrella term used to describe any artwork created today. It includes all kinds of different styles, such as installations, video art, and digital media!

Major Supreme Court Cases of the 20th Century

This chapter will explore **the major Supreme Court cases of the 20th** century that have shaped America's laws. With these thirty facts, you'll discover how these landmark decisions **protected the freedom of speech and expression,** privacy rights, and criminal justice procedures.

We'll also examine the constitutional issues surrounding each case to understand why they were so impactful.

871. **Lochner v. New York (1905):** This Supreme Court case struck down a New York law limiting the number of hours a baker could work, ruling that it violated the Due Process Clause of the Fourteenth Amendment. This case established a legal doctrine that was later widely criticized for interfering with the state's power to regulate its citizens.

872. **Muller v. Oregon (1908):** In this case, the Supreme Court upheld an Oregon law that imposed maximum working hours for women. The Supreme Court determined that the law was constitutional because it served a legitimate state interest in protecting the health of female workers. This decision established the precedent that states could pass laws regulating the health and safety of their citizens. However, it also hampered the women's rights movement for equality between the sexes.

873. **Hammer v. Dagenhart (1918):** This Supreme Court case struck down a federal law prohibiting the interstate shipment of goods produced by child labor. The Supreme Court ruled that the law violated the Constitution's Commerce Clause and was an intrusion on states' rights to regulate their citizens.

874. **Selective Draft Law Cases (1918):** In these cases, the Supreme Court upheld the constitutionality of the first peacetime military draft in the United States. The Supreme Court found that Congress had the authority to implement the draft to raise and support armies.

875. **Schenck v. United States (1919):** This Supreme Court case upheld the conviction of a man who was charged with violating the Espionage Act of 1917 for distributing literature criticizing the draft. The Supreme Court held that his actions constituted a "clear and present danger" to the nation's security. The case essentially determined that Schenck did not have the right to express his views against the draft, which violates the First Amendment.

876. **Adkins v. Children's Hospital (1923):** In this case, the Supreme Court struck down a District of Columbia law establishing a minimum wage for women. The Supreme Court held that the law violated the Due Process Clause of the Fifth Amendment because it interfered with the right to contract freely.

877. **United States v. Schwimmer (1929):** In this case, the Supreme Court held that a woman who had applied for citizenship was ineligible because she refused to take an oath of military service. The Supreme Court found that the decision to deny her application was reasonable under the Naturalization Act of 1906.

878. **Schechter Poultry Corp. v. United States (1935):** This Supreme Court case struck down a federal law that regulated the sale of poultry and other commodities. The Supreme Court found that the law exceeded Congress's power under the Commerce Clause and was an unconstitutional delegation of power.

879. **United States v. Miller (1939):** In this case, the Supreme Court held that a federal law prohibiting the interstate transportation of a sawed-off shotgun was constitutional. The Supreme Court found that the law was within Congress's power under the Commerce Clause to regulate activities that substantially affect interstate commerce.

880. United States v. Carolene Products Co. (1938): This Supreme Court case established the "footnote four" doctrine, which provides that courts should defer to laws passed by the legislature unless there is a compelling reason to do otherwise. This decision has been widely cited in subsequent cases.

881. **West Virginia State Board of Education v. Barnette (1943):** In this case, the Supreme Court held that a West Virginia law requiring schoolchildren to salute the American flag violated the First Amendment's protection of freedom of speech and expression. This decision has been widely cited as an example

882. **Korematsu v. United States (1944):** This Supreme Court case upheld the internment of Japanese Americans during World War II. The Supreme Court found that internment was a reasonable exercise of the government's power to protect national security. This decision has been widely criticized for its violation of civil liberties.

883. **Brown v. Board of Education (1954):** This Supreme Court case overturned the doctrine of "separate but equal" in public education. The Supreme Court held that racial segregation in public schools violated the Equal Protection Clause of the Fourteenth Amendment. This decision marked a major shift in the court's approach to civil rights.

884. **Mapp v. Ohio (1961):** In this case, the Supreme Court held that evidence obtained in violation of the Fourth Amendment's protection against unreasonable searches and seizures was inadmissible in criminal proceedings. This decision has been widely cited as an important protection of individual rights against government intrusion.

885. **Engel v. Vitale (1962):** The Supreme Court held that a New York law requiring public schoolchildren to recite a non-denominational prayer violated the First Amendment's Establishment Clause. This case has been widely cited as an example of the Supreme Court's protection of religious liberty.

886. **Gideon v. Wainwright (1963):** This Supreme Court case held that state and federal governments must provide legal counsel to those accused of a crime who cannot afford to hire their own lawyer. This decision marked a major shift in the Supreme Court's approach to criminal justice and has been widely cited in subsequent cases.

887. **Griswold v. Connecticut (1965):** This Supreme Court case struck down a Connecticut law prohibiting the use of contraception, finding that the law violated the right to privacy implied by the Bill of Rights. This decision marked a major shift in the Supreme Court's approach to the protection of individual rights.

888. **Miranda v. Arizona (1966):** In this case, the Supreme Court held that individuals who are taken into police custody must be informed of their right to remain silent and to have an attorney present during questioning. This case has been widely cited as an important protection of individual rights.

889. **Brandenburg v. Ohio (1969):** This Supreme Court case held that the government could not punish individuals for speech unless it is likely to incite imminent violence. This decision has been widely cited as an important protection of the right to freedom of expression.

890. **New York Times Co. v. United States (1971):**

The Supreme Court held that the First Amendment's protection of freedom of the press overruled the government's attempt to prevent the publication of classified documents. This decision has been widely cited as an important protection of the press's ability to inform the public.

891. **Furman v. Georgia (1972):** In this case, the Supreme Court held that the existing death penalty laws in the United States were unconstitutional because they were applied in an arbitrary and discriminatory manner. This decision marked a major shift in the Supreme Court's approach to capital punishment.

892. **Roe v. Wade (1973):** This Supreme Court case held that a woman's right to privacy includes the right to terminate a pregnancy. This decision marked a major shift in the Supreme Court's approach to reproductive rights and has been widely cited in subsequent cases.

893. **United States v. Nixon (1974):** In this case, the Supreme Court held that President Richard Nixon had to comply with a subpoena requesting tapes from his White House office. This decision has been widely cited as an important protection of the balance of power between the branches of government.

894. **Regents of the University of California v. Bakke (1978):** This Supreme Court case struck down a California law that established a separate admissions program for minority applicants, finding that it violated the Equal Protection Clause of the Fourteenth Amendment. This decision has been widely cited in subsequent cases.

895. **Texas v. Johnson (1989):** In this case, the Supreme Court held that the burning of an American flag was protected by the First Amendment's protection of freedom of speech and expression. This decision has been widely cited as an example of the Supreme Court's protection of individual liberty.

896. **Webster v. Reproductive Health Services (1989):** The Supreme Court upheld a Missouri law that imposed restrictions on abortion, finding that the law did not violate the right to privacy implied by the Fourteenth Amendment.

897. **United States v. Williams (1992):** The Supreme Court held that the government's ability to prosecute individuals for conspiracy to commit a crime (in this case, exchanging or selling child pornography) did not violate the First Amendment since the person would be doing something illegal anyway.

898. **United States v. Lopez (1995):** This Supreme Court case struck down a federal law that prohibited the possession of firearms within a school zone, finding that the law exceeded Congress's power under the Commerce Clause. Schools were deemed to be under the state's jurisdiction, not that of the federal government.

899. **Reno v. American Civil Liberties Union (1997):** The Supreme Court determined that communications on the internet have First Amendment protection similar to other forms of speech, meaning citizens cannot be censored online without due process.

900. **Obergefell v. Hodges (2000):** In this case, the Supreme Court stated that same-sex couples had the right to marry under the Due Process Clause and the Equal Protection Clause of the Fourteenth Amendment. This case established the right to same-sex marriage on the federal level.

African American History and Culture in the US

This chapter will explore the fascinating **history and culture of African Americans** in the United States. Through thirty interesting facts, we'll discover how enslaved Africans arrived in North America, important civil rights reforms, and influential figures like **Martin Luther King Jr.** and **Oprah Winfrey** who broke barriers for future generations.

We'll also **learn about famous African American** inventors, artists, and musicians that made an impact on our culture today. By understanding these elements of African American history, you can better appreciate their immense contributions to this nation.

901. **The first enslaved Africans arrived in Jamestown, Virginia, in 1619** aboard a Dutch trading vessel called the White Lion.

902. **Between 1525 and 1866**, 12.5 million enslaved people were brought to North America, South America, and the Caribbean from Africa.

903. **The Underground Railroad** allowed tens of thousands of African Americans to find freedom via a secret network that connected them with abolitionists willing to help them escape bondage.

904. **The infamous Dred Scott case of 1857** saw the Supreme Court decision that African Americans were not afforded the rights stated in the Constitution.

905. **The Civil War was fought from 1861 to 1865.** Although the Civil War was fought for multiple issues, the most pressing issue was keeping the institution of slavery intact in the South. During the war, President Abraham Lincoln passed the Emancipation Proclamation, freeing enslaved people in the states that had seceded.

906. In 1865, t**he Civil War was won by the North.** Several amendments, namely the Thirteenth, Fourteenth, and Fifteenth Amendments, were passed that granted and protected rights to African Americans.

907. **The period of Reconstruction took place after the Civil War.** Reconstruction had several purposes, including reuniting the country and providing a system for African Americans to get on their feet.

908. Although some steps were made in the right direction, **the Jim Crow laws** took a big step backward. Because of the laws, African Americans faced discrimination in housing, education, employment, and public accommodations.

909. **The NAACP was founded** in February 1909 by W. E. B. Du Bois, Ida B. Wells, and other activists to work for civil rights reforms.

910. **The Harlem Renaissance** was a period of artistic, literary, and musical that flourished in the 1920s and 1930s. Langston Hughes, Zora Neale Hurston, and Jacob Lawrence are some of the most renowned figures from this era.

911. **The Tuskegee Airmen** were the first black pilots to serve in the US military. They served during World War II. Their bravery and skill helped redefine the role of African Americans in the US Armed Forces.

912. In 1954, **the Supreme Court ruled that racial segregation** of schools was unconstitutional with Brown v. Board of Education. This case paved the way for the integration of education, eventually leading to more diverse classrooms across America.

913. **The Montgomery bus boycott** occurred after Rosa Parks refused to give up her seat on a bus for white passengers. This event led to the ruling that segregated buses in Alabama were unconstitutional.

914. **The 16th Street Baptist Church in Birmingham,** Alabama, was bombed by KKK members in 1963, killing four girls attending Sunday school. The KKK is a notorious hate group that has gone through multiple iterations. The group is still around today.

915. In 1964, **Martin Luther King Jr. received the Nobel Peace Prize** for his nonviolent protests against racial injustice.

916. In 1965, **President Lyndon Johnson** signed the Voting Rights Act, which outlawed many of the discriminatory voting practices used to prevent African Americans from voting, such as literacy tests and poll taxes.

917. **The Black Panthers was founded in 1966** to protect African American communities from police brutality through militant self-defense tactics. They wanted to ensure African American people could live without fear of police brutality.

918. In 1968, track athletes **John Carlos and Tommie Smith made a protest during their medal ceremony at the Summer Olympics in Mexico City** when they raised black-gloved fists during the US national anthem to show solidarity with the civil rights movement.

919. In 1968, **Martin Luther King Jr.**, a leader in the civil rights movement, was assassinated at the age of thirty-nine while standing on his hotel balcony in Memphis, Tennessee.

920. A holiday celebrating **Dr. King's legacy—Martin Luther King Day**—became an official national holiday throughout America starting in 1983.

921. In 1984, **Byllye Avery**, along with others, started the National Black Women's Health Project to educate women about health disparities in African American communities.

922. **The Million Man March** took place on October 16th, 1995. Nearly a million people from all backgrounds traveled to Washington, DC, to stand against racism and police brutality.

923. The first black president of the United States was **Barack Obama,** who served from 2009 to 2017.

924. **The Black Lives Matter movement** began after the death of Trayvon Martin when his killer, George Zimmerman, was acquitted in July 2013. The movement exploded with the deaths of Michael Brown and Eric Garner in 2014. Since then, the organization has worked toward ending violence inflicted upon black people worldwide.

925. **African American culture** is still very much alive today, with music like jazz, blues, and hip-hop being popular genres among all races.

926. **Famous African American** inventors include **Elijah McCoy** (automatic lubricator for steam engines), **George Washington Carver** (crop rotation), and **Garrett Morgan** (a kind of traffic light).

927. **Famous African Americans** that have broken barriers include **Oprah Winfrey** (media mogul), Colin Powell (the first black US Secretary of State), and **Madam C. J. Walker** (the first female self-made millionaire in America).

928. **African American authors,** such as Toni Morrison, Zora Neale Hurston, and Maya Angelou, have significantly impacted literature.

929. **African Americans** are also known for their artistry and creativity in visual arts, from painting to sculpture to photography.

930. **African American cuisine has evolved** over the years, with dishes like jambalaya, gumbo, and fried chicken being some of the most popular comfort foods.

Famous Explorers Who Founded Early Settlements in the US

This chapter will explore the fascinating **history of famous explorers** who founded early settlements in the United States. We'll take a look at thirty interesting facts about their voyages, discoveries, and contributions to American history. Furthermore, we'll examine how they utilized nature to survive in harsh conditions and developed complex trade networks between **different tribes across North America.**

931. **Leif Erikson** discovered North America centuries before Columbus, reaching Newfoundland around 1000 CE.

932. **Columbus** kicked off the start of colonization in the New World after stumbling on The Bahamas in 1492.

933. **John Cabot** claimed most of North America for England when he landed in Newfoundland in 1497.

934. **Amerigo Vespucci** explored the New World in the late 15th century and early 16th century. His name is where we get the term "America."

935. **Vasco Nuñez Balboa** crossed Panama and sighted the Pacific Ocean, becoming the first European to see it in 1513.

936. **Ponce de León discovered Florida** while allegedly searching for the Fountain of Youth in 1513. He claimed Florida for Spain and became the first known European explorer to discover what is now the United States.

937. **Giovanni da Verrazzano** sailed from France to eastern North America to search for a route to the Pacific sometime in the 1520s. He explored parts of the eastern coastline and landed near Cape Fear, North Carolina.

938. In 1524, **Estevão Gomes**, a Portuguese explorer, became the first European to discover the Hudson River. Henry Hudson would explore more of this river about ninety years later.

939. **Estevanico** was a Moroccan slave who accompanied Cabeza de Vaca on his expedition to the Southern US in 1527.

940. **Jacques Cartier** explored Canada. He notably traveled the Gulf of Saint Lawrence and the Lawrence River from 1534 to 1542.

941. **Hernando de Soto** became the first European to cross the Mississippi River in 1541.

942. **Francisco Vázquez de Coronado** led an expedition from Mexico to what is now the American Southwest in 1540 and 1542.

943. In 1542 and 1543, **Juan Rodríguez Cabrillo** became the first European to investigate modern-day California.

944. **Pedro Menéndez de Avilés** established St. Augustine as a Spanish settlement on August 28th, 1565. It is the oldest continually inhabited city in the US.

945. **Juan Pardo** established the first European settlement in North Carolina with Fort San Juan, near modern-day Morganton, in the 16th century.

946. **The English** tried to establish a permanent settlement off the coast of North Carolina in 1585. It was called **Roanoke.**

947. By 1590, the **colony of Roanoke** had been abandoned. To this day, no one is sure what happened to the colonists, although the most likely theory is that they moved to Croatoan Island.

948. **Jamestown, Virginia,** became the first permanent English settlement in America on May 14th, 1607.

949. **Samuel de Champlain** founded Quebec City and other settlements along Lake Ontario and Lake Champlain from 1608 to 1635.

950. **Henry Hudson** explored the area around what is now New York and Canada in 1609 and 1610. Hudson's men were the first Europeans to visit Hudson Bay in 1611.

951. **Hudson** was looking for the Northwest Passage, a waterway that connected the **Atlantic to the Pacific**. The Northwest Passage wouldn't be fully navigated until the early 20th century!

952. **In 1614, the Dutch established New Netherland in what is now New Jersey and New York.** The English took control of this colony sixty years later and renamed it New York.

953. **In 1620, the Pilgrims sailed the Atlantic** on the Mayflower, landing in present-day Massachusetts. They established a small colony there.

954. **Louis Joliet and Jacques Marquette** explored a huge chunk of North America on their 1673 mission. The two went from the Great Lakes region to the Gulf of Mexico.

955. **Marquette and Joliet** were also the first Europeans to explore the northern part of the Mississippi River Valley.

956. **René Robert Cavelier Sieur de La Salle** traveled along the Mississippi River, claiming much of its basin for France during 1682 and 1683.

957. From 1697 to 1702, **Eusebio Kino,** a Jesuit missionary and explorer, investigated Sonora, Mexico, and southern Arizona. He also discovered that Baja California was not an island but a peninsula.

958. In 1773, **the last of the British Thirteen Colonies** would be created. The colony of Georgia was officially established that year. It notably banned slavery and alcohol.

959. **Captain James Cook sailed for England.** He was the first European to find the Hawaiian Islands, doing so in 1778. On his third visit to the islands in 1779, he was killed by the natives.

960. **Alexander Mackenzie was the first European to cross North America** at its widest point, crossing the continent from the Pacific to the Atlantic coast via Canada's northernmost point. He accomplished this feat in 1793.

Economic Developments in the United States

This chapter will **explore economic developments in the United States.** With these facts, you'll learn how Americans have been able to achieve one of the highest per capita incomes in the world. We'll examine America's burst of economic growth and its downturn due to rising oil prices, unemployment, and inflation.

Finally, we'll discover what caused the bubbles that popped during the 2008-09 recession and look at some of the challenging issues facing the economy today.

961. **The United States has been an economic powerhouse since the late 1800s,** although it had a steady economy, for the most part, since the late 1700s.

962. During the period of 1790 to 1860, manufacturing drove much of **America's economic growth**. More factories opened, and new technologies were developed, such as Eli Whitney's cotton gin and interchangeable parts production system.

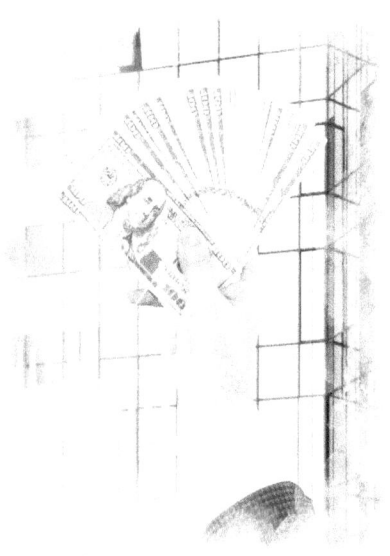

963. In the late 1800s, **after the Civil War, America saw its first real burst of economic growth** with a significant expansion of transportation and communication infrastructure, such as railroads and telegraph lines. These helped to link markets across the nation more efficiently.

964. **In 1916, the US GDP passed Britain's** due to America's technological advances in agriculture and industry that allowed for efficient mass production of products like cars and steel. Britain's economy stagnated while America's economy continued to grow.

965. **In the 1920s, the US economy boomed thanks to new inventions and technological advancements.** Assembly lines, radios, the mass production of automobiles, and the beginning of the aviation industry all contributed to the era's economic growth.

966. **After World War II ended in 1945, there was an economic boom** from 1946 through 1959 called the **"Golden Age."** Unemployment reached a record low of 2.5 percent in 1953. Incomes also raised rapidly, and there was a greater demand for consumer goods now that the war was over.

967. **In the 1950s, America's economy continued to expand** with increased manufacturing output and technological advancements. Home appliances, such as refrigerators, became more affordable for middle-class families, leading to a booming consumer market.

968. **The 1970s saw an economic downturn due to rising oil prices,** unemployment, and inflation that caused stagnation in job creation and wages. At the same time, other developed nations caught up technologically, which hurt US exports globally at the time.

969. **In the 1980s, President Ronald Reagan enacted a set of policies called "Reaganomics."** The government focused on lowering taxes for businesses and wealthy individuals and also deregulated many industries (like banking), contributing significantly toward raising economic growth rates by the early 1990s.

970. **The 1990s were considered one of the longest-running periods of uninterrupted economic expansion in American history,** thanks mainly to new technologies, such as the internet, cell phones, and computers. These items allowed people to access markets faster than ever and created tremendous opportunities for wealth.

971. **The early 2000s saw a rapid rise in housing prices,** which was fueled by low interest rates and credit access for people with poor credit histories. This led to the creation of bubbles that popped during the 2008-09 recession. The recession caused unemployment and financial distress.

972. **After the Great Recession, the US economy has been recovering,** but it still faces many problems today. For instance, the US faces income inequality, stagnant wages, rising healthcare costs, and increasing national debt levels, preventing the economy from reaching its full potential.

973. **Today, the US has the eighth-highest per capita income in the world.** On average, people in the US earn around seventy thousand dollars a year.

Cultural Events That Influenced US History

This chapter will explore **cultural events** that have shaped and **influenced US history**. These fun facts will allow you to gain more insight into **America's first Thanksgiving,** the first **St. Patrick's Day parade in New York**, and much more.

Discover how certain symbols, like the **American flag and the Statue of Liberty,** came to be and examine iconic moments, such as **the first baseball game.**

974. **The first Thanksgiving was celebrated in 1621** between the Wampanoag and English settlers of Plymouth Colony, Massachusetts.

975. **The St. Patrick's Day Parade began in New York City** on March 17th, 1762, as an Irish American celebration. Today, the holiday is celebrated around the world with parades, music, dance performances, and traditional food.

976. **The Declaration of Independence was ratified on July 4th, 1776,** declaring America's independence from Great Britain and forming a new nation. Every July 4th, Americans celebrate Independence Day with food and fireworks.

977. **The iconic American flag, the Stars and Stripes, was allegedly designed by Betsy Ross in 1776** and officially adopted on June 14th, 1777.

978. **The first baseball game played in America** is thought to have occurred between teams from New York's Knickerbocker Club and the New York Baseball Club at Elysian Fields in Hoboken, New Jersey, on June 19th, 1846.

979. **The Transcontinental Railroad connected the East Coast to the West Coast ports.** It was completed on May 10th, 1869, after six years of construction.

980. **The Battle of Gettysburg (July 1–3, 1863) between the Union and Confederate** Army marked a turning point in the Civil War. The war eventually led to the abolishment of slavery in the US.

981. **The first Labor Day Parade was held in New York City** on September 5th, 1882. Today, the first Monday of September is Labor Day, with people celebrating the holiday with parades, concerts, and other events.

982. **The Statue of Liberty is a monumental symbol of freedom and democracy.** It was gifted to the United States by France in 1885. Standing 305 feet tall, it is a reminder of the United States' commitment to liberty, justice, and equality. It has become an icon of hope and inspiration to millions around the world.

983. **The Statue of Liberty was named after Lady Liberty by French sculptor Frederic Auguste Bartholdi,** who designed the statue, which is made out of copper.

984. **Jazz music originated in New Orleans** during the late 19th century as a combination of African American music traditions with influences from European musical styles like ragtime and marching band music.

985. **Ellis Island served as an immigration station** for millions of immigrants entering America from Europe through New York Harbor beginning in 1892. It closed its doors in 1954.

986. **Women's suffrage became law** when the Nineteenth Amendment was ratified on August 18th, 1920.

987. **The National Football League (NFL)** began to play on October 3rd, 1920, making it one of the oldest professional sports leagues in the world (Major League Baseball was the first).

988. **The first American Thanksgiving Day Parade** was held in Philadelphia in 1920. The iconic New York Macy's Thanksgiving Day Parade started in 1924.

989. **The US Navy's first aircraft carrier,** USS Langley, was commissioned in 1922, ushering in a new era of military technology development.

990. **The Harlem Renaissance** was a golden age of African American artistic expression and cultural awakening that started in the 1920s and lasted until the mid-1930s.

991. **The Roaring '20s** was an exciting time in US history. Everything from politics to music and dancing saw changes.

992. On March 3rd, 1932, **President Herbert Hoover** declared **"The Star-Spangled Banner"** by Francis Scott Key to be America's national anthem.

993. **President Franklin D. Roosevelt's** New Deal legislation during the 1930s provided funds for public works projects, welfare reform, and bank regulation, among other measures, to help America recover from the Great Depression.

994. In 1947, **America's first drive-thru** opened: Red's Giant Hamburg in Missouri. Today, there are over 200,000 drive-thrus in the country!

995. In 1955, **Rosa Parks refused to give up her seat on the bus for a white passenger,** sparking the Montgomery bus boycott.

996. **Hawaii became part of the US** on August 21st, 1959. Hawaii became the fiftieth state of the US.

997. On August 28th, 1963, **Martin Luther King Jr. delivered his famous "I Have a Dream"** speech at the end of the March on Washington for Jobs and Freedom. The march and the speech became a defining moment of the civil rights movement, inspiring people all around the globe.

998. On June 28th, 1969, **police raids against members of the LGBTQ community at Stonewall Inn in New York City** triggered protests and riots that launched the modern gay rights movement in US history.

999. In July 1969, **Neil Armstrong became the first man to walk on the moon,** ending the Space Race. This was an incredible feat, and people all over the world tuned in to watch the momentous occasion.

1000. **Woodstock was a three-day concert that promoted peace and love**. Iconic musicians like **Jimi Hendrix, Janis Joplin, Jefferson Airplane,** and more performed near Bethel, New York, in mid-August 1969, attracting almost 500,000 people!

Conclusion

After reading **one thousand interesting facts about American history**, it should be easy to see how much the country has evolved over the years. Not only have you become more knowledgeable on an array of topics related **to American history**, but hopefully, **this book** has also inspired a newfound appreciation for the events and people that shaped America into **what it is today!**

To continue your journey and learn even **more about America's past**, take advantage of the resources listed in the bibliography. Also, make sure to keep an eye out for more **books in this series!**

Sources and Additional References

Thornton, Russell. American Indian Holocaust and Survival: A Population History Since 1492. University of Oklahoma Press, 2015.

Thornton, Russell. The Cherokees: A Population History. University of Nebraska Press, 1990.

White, Bruce M. The Stone Age of the Great Lakes. University of Michigan Press, 1965.

King, Mary Elizabeth. Ceramics for the Archaeologist. Smithsonian Institution Press, 1975.

Smith, Andrea. Native Americans: A History. St. Martin's Press, 2011.

Kickingbird, Kirke, and Herbert T. Hoover. Indian Traders of the Southeastern Spanish Borderlands: Panton, Leslie & Company and John Forbes & Company, 1783-1847. University of Oklahoma Press, 2011.

Kostiainen, Vaino. The Development of American Agriculture: A Historical Analysis. University of Minnesota Press, 2008.

Anderson, Carol. The Indian Way: Learning to Communicate with Mother Earth. Santa Fe, NM: Sunstone Press, 2014.

Dominguez, Virgil. Native American Art in the Twentieth Century. Austin, TX: University of Texas Press, 1998.

White, Richard. The Middle Ground: Indians, Empires, and Republics in the Great Lakes Region, 1650-1815. Cambridge: Cambridge University Press, 1991.

Sault, Carole A. Native American Medicine. ABC-CLIO, Inc., 2000.

Orenstein, Ruth M. Native American History. Greenwood Press, 1996.

Deloria, Vine, Jr. and David E. Wilkins. American Indian Politics and the American Political System. Rowman & Littlefield, 2000.

Mohawk, John. Native American Spirituality. Viking, 1993.

Orenstein, Ruth M. American Indian Arts and Crafts. Greenwood Press, 1994.

Nelson, S. The Role of Medicine Men and Women in Native American Culture. The Rosen Publishing Group, 2011.

Ross, David. Buffalo Hunt: Native American Hunting and the Sacred Buffalo. Capstone Press, 2007.

Stein, Rob. Native American Migration Patterns. Facts on File, 2006.

Dunn, Jill. Native American Sustainable Agriculture Practices. The Rosen Publishing Group, 2010.

Bierhorst, John. Native American Spirituality: A Critical Reader. University of Arizona Press, 2008.

Stone, Lynn M. American Indian History: An Introduction. ABC-CLIO, 2015.

"Exploring America: The Story of the U.S.A.". Raintree, 2014.

"Jamestown Settlement." Encyclopedia Virginia, http://encyclopediavirginia.org/Jamestown_Settlement#start_entry.

Taylor, Alan. The Civil War of 1812: American Citizens, British Subjects, Irish Rebels, & Indian Allies. Vintage, 2012.

Helgerson Richard L., et al., eds. "Spanish Exploration and Settlement in North America (1492–1763)." The Oxford Companion to United States History, Oxford University Press, 2001; accessed April 28 2020 from Encyclopedia Britannica online: https://www.britannica.com/topic/list-of-SpaniardsettlementsinNorthAmerica.

"Dutch Colonies in North America (1609–74)." Encyclopedia Britannica, March 15 2019; Accessed April 28 2020 from https://www.britannica.com/topic/list-of-Dutchcoloniesinnorthamericahistory.

Bradford, William. Of Plymouth Plantation. Edited by Samuel Eliot Morison, Alfred A. Knopf, 2020.

Weber, David J. The Spanish Frontier in North America. Yale University Press, 1992.

Robinson, Donald L., ed. Slavery in the Structure of American Politics, 1765-1820. Harcourt Brace Jovanovich, 1971.

Wood, Gordon S. The American Revolution: A History. Modern Library, 2002.

Foner, Eric. Give Me Liberty!: An American History. W. W. Norton & Company, 2017.

McConnell, M. A Country of Vast Designs: James K. Polk, the Mexican War and the Conquest of the American Continent. New York, NY: Simon & Schuster, 2016.

Gerson, Noel B. The Northwest Ordinance: A Bicentennial Handbook. Scarecrow Press, 1987.

Ambrosius, Lloyd E. Woodrow Wilson and the American Diplomatic Tradition: The Treaty Fight in Perspective. Cambridge University Press, 1991.

Gilderhus, Mark T. The Second Century: U.S.-Latin American Relations Since 1889. Routledge, 2006.

Estes, Todd. Acquiring America: The Acquisition of Florida and the Formation of the United States, 1819-1845. The University of Georgia Press, 2003.

Faragher, John Mack. Rereading Frederick Jackson Turner: "The Significance of the Frontier in American History" and Other Essays. Yale University Press, 1998.

Miller, Charles P. The United States and Latin America: Myths and Stereotypes of Civilization and Nature. University of Texas Press, 1992.

Murray, Robert K., and Rudolph M. Bell. The Social Meaning of the Great Awakening in America: Religion's Changing Role in American Life 1620-1860. Rutgers University Press, 1992.

Berger, Thomas A., eds. Jonathan Edwards and the Baptists: Guiding the Way to a New Age of Revivalism and Activism. Mercer Univ Pr, 2009.

"Great Awakening." Encyclopedia Britannica Online School Edition, Encyclopedia Britannica Inc., 2020.

Hall, David D., eds. The Cambridge History of Religion in America: Volume 2 From the Great Awakening to the Revolution. Cambridge University Press, 2011.

McGlone, Robert E. George Whitefield and the Rise of Modern Evangelicalism. Baker Academic, 2004.

Bailyn, Bernard. The Ideological Origins of the American Revolution. Harvard Univ Pr, 1992.

Kidd, Thomas S., and Barry Hankins. The Great Awakening: The Roots of Evangelical Christianity in Colonial America. Yale University Press, 2007.

Haller Jr., William H. "The Age of Reason in American History." Annals Of Science 30 (1973): 1–14.

Price, Peter M., et al. Enlightenment & Reform in Eighteenth-Century Europe. Cambridge University Press, 2016.

Thiessen, Richard C., and James K. Dew Jr. American Religious History: A Very Short Introduction. Oxford University Press, 2016.

"The French and Indian War." Encyclopedia Britannica, edited by Robert W. Smith, 27th ed., vol. 5, Encyclopedia Britannica, Inc., 2021, pp. 589-590.

Tucker, Spencer C. The Encyclopedia of North American Indian Wars 1607-1890: A Political, Social, and Military History. ABC-CLIO, 2011.

Arnade, Charles W. "The French and Indian War and Its Impact on American History." The French and Indian War: Deciding the Fate of North America, edited by John E. Ferling, Greenwood Press, 2000, pp. 79-97.

Farnham, Thomas J. "The French and Indian War: A History of Its Causes and Consequences." The French and Indian War: Deciding the Fate of North America, edited by John E. Ferling, Greenwood Press, 2000, pp. 1-20.

Edmonds, J. E. The French and Indian War 1754-1763. New York: Routledge, 2002.

Anderson, Fred. Crucible of War: The Seven Years' War and the Fate of Empire in British North America, 1754-1766. New York: Vintage Books, 2001.

Thomas, David. The French and Indian War: Deciding the Fate of North America. New York: Rosen, 2013.

Brown, Jonathan. The Seven Years' War and the Old Regime in France: The Economic and Social Consequences of a Systematic Military Mobilization. Palgrave Macmillan, 2016.

Starkey, Armstrong. European and Native American Warfare, 1675-1815. University of Oklahoma Press, 1998.

Encyclopedia Britannica. "Seven Years' War." Encyclopedia Britannica, Encyclopedia Britannica, Inc., 2006.

Merrell, James H. "Ohio Valley." The Oxford Companion to United States History, edited by Paul S. Boyer, Oxford University Press, 2001, p. 654.

Henry, Christi. The American Revolution: A Primary Source History of the War for Independence. Rosen Pub., 2009.

Kunhardt, Dorothy Meserve and Philip B. Jr. Washington in the American Revolution: 1775-1783 New York: Harcourt Brace Jovanovich, c1976., 1976.

Grant, James P. The Forgotten Founders on Religion and Public Life Notre Dame, IN: University of Notre Dame Press; 2009., 2009. Print.

Ellis, Joseph J. Founding Brothers: The Revolutionary Generation New York: Alfred A. Knopf, 2000., 2000.

Brault, Gerry. The American Revolution: War for Independence (American Heritage). Minneapolis: Twenty-First Century Books, 2007. Print.

"No Taxation without Representation." The American Revolution: Primary Sources, edited by Christine A. Norton et al., Macmillan Reference USA, 2006, pp. 157-158.

Bremer, Francis J., ed. Empire or Independence: A Revolutionary Struggle 1763–1776. Routledge, 2015.

Allen Campbell Miller and John C Miller III, The American Revolution: Writings from the War of Independence (New York; Library Classics of the United States Incorporated 2016).

Smith Robert R et al Boston Tea Party Ships & Museum Visitors Guide (Boston; Historic Tours of America 2019).

Daniels, Kate and Karen Bush Gibson (eds.). Our American Revolution: Seven Stories of Courage That Changed the Nation. National Geographic Society, 2019.

"Paul Revere's Ride." American Revolution, edited by Diane Yancey, Greenhaven Press, 2007.

Weintraub, Stanley. Washington: A Life. Penguin Books USA Inc., 2011.

"Patrick Henry's Give Me Liberty or Give Me Death Speech" The Revolutionary War in the

United States of America 1775–1783, Britannica Educational Publishing in Association with Rosen Educational Services LLC., 2015.

Zinn, Howard. A People's History of the United States: 1492 to Present. HarperCollins Publishers, 2005.

Paine, Thomas. Common Sense and Other Writings by Thomas Paine Penguin Books Ltd., 1986.

"The Articles of Confederation: Establishing the United States Government." The U.S. Constitution, edited by Jack E. Frazier, Greenhaven Press/Gale Cengage Learning, 2011.

Waldstreicher, David et al., eds. A Companion to the American Revolution: Blackwell Companions to American History Series. Wiley-Blackwell -John Wiley [and] Sons Incorporated, 2004.

Ketchum, Richard M. Victory at Yorktown: The Campaign That Won the Revolution. Henry Holt and Co., 2004.

Schama, Simon, Rough Crossings: Britain, the Slaves and the American Revolution. Ecco Press/HarperCollins Publishers Ltd., 2006.

McBride, Amanda. Women of the American Revolution: An Illustrated History. Pelican Publishing Company, Inc., 2018.

Boorstin, Julia, The Many Lives of Betsy Ross: Woman Behind the Legend. National Geographic Society, 2019.

Smith, John. The Battle of Monmouth: A Revolutionary War Turning Point. Greenhaven Press, 2013.

Gerson, Carole B., and Sarah E Anderson. The Boston Massacre: Five Colonists Killed by British Soldiers in 1770 Spark a Revolution! Enslow Publishing LLC, 2008.

Thomas Jefferson's Virginia Statute for Religious Freedom: Its Evolution and Consequences in American History. New York University Press, 2010.

Furtwangler, Albert. The Constitutional Convention and Formation of the Union. Oxford University Press, 2017.

"Founding Fathers." World Book Encyclopedia, vol. 8, World Book, 2019, pp. 49-50.

Rosen, Jeffrey. Our Constitution: How It Works and Why It Endures. New York: Oxford University Press, 2018.

Atkins, Stephen. The American Constitution: Its Origins and Development. 8th ed., Vol. 2, W.W. Norton & Company, Inc., 2009.

Jone Johnson Lewis, Understanding American Government & Politics: What You Need to Know About Our System of Government & Politics (Washington Dc.: National Geographic Learning Cengage Learning, 2019), 21-22.

U.S Constitution: The Essential Companion. Edited by Michael Arnheim and Linda Monk, Oxford University Press, 2018.

Alexander Hamilton Institute (US). The Constitution for Everyone: How Americans Interpreted Their Most Powerful Document from 1789 to the Present Day, Skyhorse Publishing Inc., 2020.

Rossiter, Clinton L. ed., The Federalist Papers (signet Classics). Penguin Books Ltd., 2003.

"Making Sense of the US Constitution". PBS Learning Media LLC., 2017.

"The US Constitution: Its History and Promise". National Archives & Records Administration, 2019.

United States. Constitution of the United States of America: With a Summary of the Actions by the States in Ratification Thereof, and an Appendix Containing

Important Documents and Records, Together with Notes and Commentaries on Its Provisions. U.S Government Printing Office, 1897.

"George Washington." Biography Online, biographyonline.net/us-presidents/george-washington-1732-99/.

Ellis, Joseph J. His Excellency George Washington: The Indispensable Man as You've Never Seen Him Before. Penguin Press HC, 2004.

Chernow, Ron. Washington: A Life. Penguin Group (USA), Inc., 2010.

Leiner, Fredric. George Washington: A Biographical Companion. ABC-CLIO, Inc., 2002.

Ferling, John E. The Ascent of George Washington: The Hidden Political Genius of an American Icon. Bloomsbury Press USA, 2009.

Kissinger, William F. George Washington: An American Icon. Greenwood Publishing Group, 2004.

Brown, Carter Smith. George Washington: The Making of the Nation's First President. ABC-CLIO, 2015.

Ferling, John E. Setting the World Ablaze: George Washington & The American Revolution. Oxford University Press Inc., 2000.

Unrau, Harlan D. George Washington and the Politics of Knowledge. University Press of Kansas, 2008.

Rees, David J. George Washington: Hero of the American Revolution. Gareth Stevens Publishing, 2016.

Burt, Arnold S. The United States in the War of 1812: An Encyclopedia. Routledge, 2014.

Heidler, David Stephen and Jeanne T., eds., Encyclopedia of the War of 1812 Santa Barbara: ABC-CLIO, Inc., 2012.

Mackesy, Piers "The Second War of Independence" Military History Aug 2015.

Kallen, Stuart A., and Jody S. Feldman. The War of 1812: Conflict between America and Great Britain (High Five Reading - Blue Level). Lerner Publications Company, 2017.

Smith-Christopher, Daniel L. Understanding the War of 1812: A Student Companion (Oxford Student Companions to American History). Oxford University Press, 2001.

Miller, Roger G. The War of 1812: A Forgotten Conflict (The Library of American Military History). University Of Illinois Press, 2012.

Howe, John R., and Stuart Fickling. The War of 1812: A Short History. Oxford University Press, 2018 p. 10.

Cresswell, Stephen E., The War of 1812: Conflict for a Continent (Campaigns & Commanders), Osprey Publishing Ltd., 2013.

McClellan III, Edwin S. The War Of 1812: An Overview and Analysis of America's Second War with Great Britain from Multiple Perspectives. McFarland & Co Inc Publ, 2017.

Ratner, Lorman. The War of 1812: A Reference Handbook. ABC-CLIO, 2007.

"The Indian Removal Act." The American Journey: A History of the United States, vol. 1, by Joyce Oldham Appleby et al., Pearson Education Inc., 2018, pp. 345-346.

"The Indian Removal Act of 1830." Native American History: An Encyclopedia, vol. 2, edited by Bruce E. Johansen, ABC-CLIO LLC., 2001, pp. 561-564.

Jacobs, Margaret D., ed. The Routledge Handbook of American Indian History. Taylor & Francis Group LLC, 2018.

O'Brien, Jean M., and Larry Nesper. The American Indian Experience: A Sourcebook on the History of Native Americans from Precontact to the Present. ABC-CLIO, 2015.

National Park Service, U.S. Department of the Interior. "The Trail of Tears National Historic Trail." National Parks Service, https://www.nps.gov/trte/index.htm.

Johnson, Troy R., and Nancy J Veenkamp (eds.). The Indian Removal Act: A Primary

Source Investigation into the Forced Relocation of Native Americans in the 1830s. Greenhaven Press, 2007.

"The Indian Removal Act." Native American Tribes, edited by David Jeffery, Chelsea House Publishers, 2010, pp. 258-260.

Forsyth, Lisa. "The Indian Removal Act of 1830." Encyclopedia of Native American Wars and Warfare, edited by Paul S. Boyer et al., Facts on File, 2005, pp. 199-201.

Calloway Colin G. The Cherokee Nation & the Trail of Tears. Penguin Books Ltd., 2007, p. 143.

"The Civil War." American History, edited by Robert J. Maddox et al., vol. 2, ABC-CLIO, 2016, pp. 816–818.

"Abraham Lincoln and the End of Slavery," American History: UXL Encyclopedia of U S History, edited by David M Neely et al., vol 3. Gale Cengage Learning 2009, pp 586–587.

McPherson, James M. Battle Cry of Freedom: The Civil War Era. Oxford University Press, 1988.

Davis, William C., and James I Robertson Jr. The Civil War: A Complete Military History. Skyhorse Publishing Inc., 2011.

Martin, David G. Gettysburg July 1st 1863: Union & Confederate Tactics & Troop Movements Illustrated in Color Maps. Stackpole Books, 2008.

Bancroft, Frederic. The Emancipation Proclamation. New York: Dodd, Mead and Company, 1883.

Bearss, Edwin C., and Stanley F Horn. The Road to Appomattox Court House: A Sourcebook on the Civil War. Savas Beatie, 2008.

The Thirteenth Amendment of the United States Constitution: Slavery and Involuntary Servitude, ed. William B White (New York: Oxford University Press, 2016).

Johnson, Paul D., Civil War America: Voices from the Home Front (Santa Barbara CA: ABC CLIO LLC, 2020).

Davis Jr., William C. Battle at Bull Run: A history of the first major campaign of the Civil War (1st Da Capo Press pbk ed.). Cambridge MA; London: Da Capo Press, 2002.

McPherson James M. Crossroads Of Freedom: Antietam (Oxford Paperbacks Ed.). New York, Oxford Univ Pr. (2001).

Olsen, Eric A. Great Plains Ranchers & the Mythic Cowboy of the Old West: Cowboys in Montana and North Dakota History (1850–1920). McFarland & Company Inc., 2012.

Taylor, Alan. American Colonies: The Settling of North America. Penguin Books Ltd., 2003.

Smith, David C., and Lise Mitchell. The Westward Expansion: A History of the American Frontier. ABC-CLIO, 2019.

The Transcontinental Railroad, 1863-1869. Ed., Nelson E. Limerick and Richard White. New York: Oxford University Press, 2011.

Jesse James: Legendary Outlaw of the Old West, by William B Thorndike Jr. Minneapolis: Compass Point Books, 2005.

Cowboy Gear: A Photographic Portrayal of the Early Cowboys and Their Equipment, ed., David R Wagner. Norman: University of Oklahoma Press, 2001.

U S cavalry vs Native Americans in the American West 1866–1916, by Robert M Utley. San Diego: Lucent Books Incorporated, 2007.

Gold Rush Towns in California and Alaska from Boom to Bust!, by Charles W Carey Jr. Berkeley Heights NJ: Enslow Publishers Inc., 2012.

Miller, Brandon Marie. Cowboys on the Frontier: An American History of Cattle Drives, Cowboy Life, and Western Expansion. Capstone Classroom, 2018.

Ball, Larry D., and Stuart A. Kallen. The Wild West: From Cowboys to Buffalo Bill (Defining Moments). Abdo Publishing Company, 2011.

LaRocque, Pauline Sangreye. Gunslingers: Famous Outlaws & Lawmen of the Wild West (The Mythic World of.). Capstone Press, 2007.

Gordon, Sharon K. Cowboys and Cow Towns of the Wild West (Santa Barbara, CA: Greenwood Publishing Group, 2005), 78.

Endreson Jr., Fritiof T., The Buffalo Soldiers and Officers of the Ninth Cavalry 1867-1898 (Jefferson City MO: McFarland & Company Incorporated Publishers, 2015), 7-8.

Anderson, William G., and Eugene C. Murdock. The Wild West: A History of the American Frontier. ABC-CLIO, 2010.

Millar, Andrew J. The Industrial Revolution: A Very Short Introduction. Oxford University Press, 2016.

Caron, Jean Baptiste and Charles Louis Cadet de Gassicourt. An Essay on the History of the Steam Engine in Europe and America During the Eighteenth Century: With a Memoir of Its Author--Jean Baptiste Caron (1790). Forgotten Books, 2017.

Cole, Heather A., and Eric B. Shiraev. The Industrial Revolution: History in an Hour Series. HarperCollins UK, 2011.

Haywood, John M., and Alan McGowan. The Routledge Companion to the Industrial Revolution in World History (Routledge Companions). Taylor & Francis Group LLC., 2017.

Anderson, Robert C. The Industrial Revolution: A Very Short Introduction. Oxford University Press, 2018.

Colman, Andrew and Bill Fawcett, eds., Encyclopedia of the Industrial Revolution in World History (Santa Barbara: ABC-CLIO/Greenwood Publishing Group Inc., 2017).

"Spanish-American War." World Book Encyclopedia, 2017 ed., vol. 22, p. 567.

Gaffney Jr., Timothy D. America's Small Wars: A Reference Guide from 1798 to the Present Westport, CT: Greenwood Press, 2006, p. 109.

Harrold, Stanley C., and Martin P. Snyder. The Spanish-American War: A Brief History with Documents. Bedford/St Martins, 2006.

Hickey, Donald R. The War of 1898: The US and Spain in History and Memory. Univ of North Carolina Press, 1998.

Smith, Justin Harvey., et al., eds A History of the Spanish-American War: A Nation Emerges from Conflict. ABC-CLIO LLC., 2019.

Winter, Frank H. The First Great War of the World: A History of the Spanish-American War and Its Consequences. McFarland & Company, Inc., Publishers., 2016.

Miller, John J. The Spanish-American War and Philippine Insurrection 1898-1902. Brassey's Inc., 1997.

Strachan, Hew. The Oxford Illustrated History of the First World War. Oxford University Press, 2001.

Hart, Stephen A. The Great War: World War I and the American Century. University of Nebraska Press, 2013.

Breen, William J. "American Military Participation in World War I." The American Historical Review, vol. 92, no. 3, 1987, pp. 617–649., doi:10.2307/1876015.

Gallagher, Gary W. The American Experience in World War I. Bloomsbury Academic, 2005, p. 87.

Davis, Lynn E. World War I: The American Soldier Experience. ABC-CLIO, 2011, p. 63.

Miller, Edward S., et al., eds. Naval History and Heritage Command: U S Navy in the Great War (WWI). Government Printing Office, 2014, p 25-26.

Wilson, Woodrow. "The 14 Points." The White House: A Brief History of the President's Home, by William Seale, National Geographic Society, 2004, pp. 49-51.

Gardner, W.J R., ed. The Allied Navies in World War II: A Complete Illustrated History of the Naval Wars 1939-1945 From All Nations Involved (Cassell Military Classics). Cassell & Co., 2006.

Rosenberg, Jennifer D. World War I: The Definitive Encyclopedia and Document Collection. ABC-CLIO, 2017.

Keegan, John. The First World War. Vintage Books, 2000.

The Oxford Encyclopedia of Women in World History. "Nineteenth Amendment to the U.S Constitution." 2008 ed., vol. 3, Oxford University Press, 2008, pp. 418-419.

DuBois, Ellen Carol and Linda Gordon editors "The Reader's Companion to U.S Women's History" Houghton Mifflin Harcourt Publishing Company New York 1998 pp 486-487.

Cott, Nancy F. The Grounding of Modern Feminism: Harvard University Press 1987 p82.

Murphy, Jane Marie editor "Women's Suffrage in America: An Eyewitness History" Facts on File New York 2009 p. 10.

O'Neal, Rick et al editors 'Encyclopedia of American Social Movements" (Routledge 2004) p. 690.

Breen, Margaret A., and Maria T. Bruce. The Women's Suffrage Movement in America: A Reference Guide 1866-1920. Greenwood Press, 2003.

Foner, Nancy Hewitt ed. Not for Ourselves Alone: The Story of Elizabeth Cady Stanton and Susan B. Anthony. New York: Viking Penguin Books Inc., 1999.

Brown, Sally. Women's Suffrage in the United States: An Eyewitness History. Routledge, 2012.

"The 19th Amendment." Our Documents: 100 Milestone Documents from the National Archives, by Paul Finkelman and Donald Ritchie, Oxford Univ. Press, 2017.

Levine-Keating, Emily S., et al. Women's Suffrage in America: An Encyclopedia of People, Issues Events and Organizations (2 vol.). ABC-CLIO, 2018.

Smith, Jeff. The Roaring Twenties: A History from Beginning to End. Hourly History, 2018.

McPherson, Stephanie Sammartino and James Buckley Jr. The Roaring Twenties: 1920s Popular Culture & the Jazz Age (American History). 100% Education Inc., 2013.

"Women's Suffrage." The New Book of Knowledge, Grolier Online Academic Edition, edited by Ann-Marie Imbornoni et al., vol. 20: People in History and the World Around Us, Scholastic Inc., 2019.

"The Roaring Twenties." The New Book of Knowledge, Grolier Online Academic Edition, edited by Ann-Marie Imbornoni et al., vol. 20: People in History and the World Around Us, Scholastic Inc., 2019.

Rice-Jones Radcliffe Institute for Advanced Study Harvard University eds. Insulin 100 Years: A Revolution in Diabetes Care, Oxfordshire UK: CABI Publishing (2014).

Zuckerman, Gregory. The Roaring Twenties: A Historical Snapshot of America's Jazz Age. ABDO Publishing Company, 2009.

Clavin, Matthew and Stephen Minger. Babe Ruth: Baseball Superstar and American Icon. Chelsea House Publishers, 2006.

Lindbergh Charles A. The Spirit of St Louis: Autobiography of Charles A Lindbergh. Scribner, 1953.

Kostyal Karmen M. Al Capone: Chicago Gangster (Famous Figures Of The Jazz Age).

National Geographic Society, 2014.

Blumberg, Rhoda. The Roaring Twenties: A History of the Decade That Shaped America. New York: Facts on File, Inc., 2002.

"The Great Depression." History, edited by Susan Ware, vol. 3: American Encounters and Global Interactions since 1750, ABC-CLIO, 2016, pp. 748-749.

Robert Siegel and David Kennedy eds., The Great Depression Encyclopedia (Santa Barbara: ABC-CLIO Incorporated, 2011), 517–518.

"Relief and Reform Programs of the New Deal." The Great Depression: An Encyclopedia of the Worst Financial Crisis in U S History, edited by Maury Klein et al., ABC-CLIO/Greenwood, 2008, pp 270-272.

"The Great Depression." American History Online Resource Center, Gale Group Inc., 2000.

Ellwood, Chris. The Great Depression: A History in Documents. Oxford University Press, 2003.

Kirn, Walter. Undaunted: The Forgotten Giants of the Great Depression Mill City Press 2012.

Tugwell, Rexford G. The Democratic Roosevelt: A Biography of Franklin D. Roosevelt. Garden City, NY: Doubleday and Company Inc., 1957.

Harvard Law Review Association. The Labor Relations Act of 1935. Cambridge, MA: Harvard University Press, 1936.

Price, Daryll E., ed. Dust Bowl Descent. Lincoln: The University of Nebraska Press, 2007.

Tennessee Valley Authority. Nashville TN: TVA Publications, 2017.

Moehling, Carolyn M. "The Great Depression and the Social Security Act of 1935." The Journal of Economic Perspectives, vol. 22, no 4., 2008, pp 133-156.

Eisenhower, John S. D-Day: June 6, 1944: The Climactic Battle of World War II. Simon & Schuster, 2019.

Weigley, Russell F. The American Way of War: A History of United States Military Strategy and Policy. Indiana University Press; Reissue edition (September 1, 2014).

Schomburg, Robert and Christopher Schomburg. World War II: A Global History of the Greatest Conflict in Human History. ABC-CLIO (2019): p47.

Smith, Michael Stephen., U S Army In WWII: European Theater of Operations Combat Arms Regimental System from 1944 to 1945. Naval Institute Press (2012).

Skidmore, Max J., and Thomas E. Baker. The G.I. Bill: A New Deal for Veterans (American Milestones). ABDO Publishing Company, 2009.

Holmquist-Wall, Leslie J., and Anne M Hussey Smithfield Middle School Students, The Manhattan Project (We the People: Modern America). Lerner Publications Co. 2009.

Karpinski, Joanne Mattern. Lend Lease Act of 1941 (America at War). Capstone Press 2012.

Miller, Nathan. War at Sea: A Naval History of World War II. Oxford University Press, 1995, p. 415.

O'Brien, David M., ed. American Military History: Volume II – The United States Army in a Global Era 1917-2003. CQ Press, 2009, p. 394.

Abeyta, Robert R. "Japanese American Internment During World War II." Gale Encyclopedia of Multicultural America 3rd Edition Detroit: Gale Cengage Learning, 2014.

O'Brien, Robert F., and Harry W. Bauer. The Battle of Iwo Jima: Victory in the Pacific. ABC-CLIO, 2007.

Keegan, John. Six Armies in Normandy: From D-Day to the Liberation of Paris June 6th -

August 25th 1944. Penguin Books Ltd., 1983.

Gaddis, John Lewis. The Cold War: A New History. Penguin Press, 2005.

Bridgeman, Harriet and David Salariya. Space Exploration Through the Ages. QEB Publishing Ltd., 2018.

National Aeronautics and Space Administration, "A Short History of NASA," https://history.nasa.gov/nltr17-4.htm, Accessed March 12th 2021.

Ryan Somma, Exploring the Moon: The Apollo Expeditions (New York: Dover Publications Inc., 2018), 32-33.

Birdsell, Susan Nacev and David Haines. Cold War Bunker Culture from Manhattan to Moscow. Gainesville FL: University Press of Florida, 2013.

Litovkin Eugene G., Vyacheslav Dokuchaev et al. Underground Cities for Nuclear War Survival: Designing Constructing & Operating Bunkers for Civil Defense Planning. New York NY: Springer Science+Business Media LLC, 2012.

Anderson Bill with Patrick O'Connor eds. Olympics Games Rivalry between the United States and Russia: A History of Mutual Respect. New York NY: Palgrave Macmillan, 2017.

White, Stephen. Cold War: A Very Short Introduction. Oxford University Press, 2017.

Leffler, Melvyn P., and Odd Arne Westad. The Cambridge History of the Cold War: Volume 1, Origins. Cambridge University Press, 2010.

Chait, Gregory. The Space Race: An Exploration of the History and Technology Behind It. Rosen Publishing Group, 2009.

Korte Barbara C., et al. Cold War America 1945 to 1991: A Documentary Reader. Oxford University Press, 2014.

McPherson, James M. The Struggle for Equality: A History of the Civil Rights Movement. Princeton University Press, 2014.

Miller, LaDonna C., and Dorothy Waugh Coulter, eds. African American History in America: From Slavery to Freedom [and Beyond]. ABC-CLIO eBook Collection (ABC-CLIO), 2010.

Pemberton, William E., Jr. Rosa Parks: A Biography. Greenwood Publishing Group, 2006.

Mays, Benjamin E., and Joseph Waddell Tupeney III. The Essential Martin Luther King Jr.: "I Have a Dream" and Other Great Writings by Martin Luther King Jr. New American Library Trade Paperbacks, 2001.

U.S. Congress. Voting Rights Act of 1965, Pub L 89-110, 79 Stat 437 (1965).

U.S Congress Fair Housing Act of 1968, 42 USCA § 3601 et seq., Title VIII of the Civil Rights Act (1968).

Hamilton, Virginia Storrs., The Little Rock Nine: Brave Students Who Desegregated Central High School (Graphic Library). Capstone Press, 2007.

"March on Washington for Jobs and Freedom," National Park Service U.S Department of Interior Accessed 30 April 2021.

Katz, Friedrich E. The Life and Times of Cesar Chavez. Univ of California Press, 2007.

Johnson, Troy R., and Stephen E. Cornell. The Occupation of Alcatraz Island: Indian Self Determination and the Rise of Indian Activism. University of Arizona Press, 1996.

Baskin, Barbara A., and Kathleen M. Brown-Pérez. Rosa Parks and the Montgomery Bus Boycott: Brave Words at a Bold Stand. Enslow Pub Incorporated, 2012.

Duberman, Martin., Martha Vicinus., and George Chauncey Jr. Hidden from History: Reclaiming the Gay & Lesbian Past. New York: Meridian Books, 1990.

Martin, Thomas D., ed. The Oxford Handbook of the Civil Rights Movement. Oxford University Press, 2015.

O'Brien, Ashley J., and Lawrence J. Korb. The Gulf War: An Encyclopedia. ABC-CLIO, 2015.

Robert C Pascoe Jr., The War on Terror Encyclopedia (Santa Barbara, CA: ABC-CLIO, 2012), pp. xxi–xxii.

Chirico, Matthew A. Global Terrorism: Origins, Dynamics and Responses. Palgrave Macmillan, 2014.

Johnson, Chalmers A., and James Fallows. The Limits of Power: The End of American Exceptionalism. Metropolitan Books, 2008.

Hakimzadeh, Sanam Vakil et al eds. US Foreign Policy in the Middle East: From Bush to Obama and Beyond. Routledge Taylor & Francis Group, 2016.

Smith, Robert W., II et al eds. After 9/11: Civil Liberties in a Time of Crisis. Prometheus Books 2007.

Merom, Gil. How Terrorism Ends: Understanding the Decline and Demise of Terrorist Campaigns. Princeton University Press, 2009.

Flagel, Aaron J., ed., The Routledge Companion to the War on Terror (Routledge Companions). Routledge Taylor & Francis Group, 2013.

Hayes, Stephen M., ed. Global Terrorism: Prevalence of Domestic & International Terrorists Motives & Tactics Today. ABC CLIO LLC, 2018.

Albrecht, Holger. The United Nations and Conflict Resolution: Security Policies in Practice. Oxford University Press, 2016.

"Human Rights Violations in the War on Terror." Stanford Law Review 58 (2006): 1363-1395.

Bergen, Peter L., Beverley Gaudet and Margo Eanett Simonsen After 9/11: An Oral History of the Attacks – Their Aftermath & the War on Terror from those who were there 1st ed., Free Press; Reprint edition 2010.

Summers Jr., Harry G., and Ernest Wiltse van Dyke III. America at War since 1945: Politics and Diplomacy in Korea, Vietnam, and the Gulf War Era. Rowman & Littlefield Education Incorporated, 2008.

Roubini, Nouriel. The Global Economy Today. McGraw-Hill Education, 2017.

Cooper, Richard N., et al. America for Beginners. Oxford University Press, 2012.

Barlett, Donald L., and James B. Steele. America: What Went Wrong? Andrews McMeel Publishing, 2012.

"Total Solar Eclipse Casts Shadow Across United States." World Book, 2017.

Bamford, James. The Shadow Factory: The Ultra-Secret NSA from 9/11 to the Eavesdropping on America. Anchor, 2009.

"Hurricane Katrina." World Book, 2016.

Obergefell v. Hodges, 576 U.S. (2015).

Bradsher, Keith. "The Future of Technology Is Now." National Geographic, vol. 230, no. 2, Feb. 2017, pp. 38-63.

Fuchs, Andreas. Obama: The Story of Barack Obama. Skyhorse Publishing, 2019.

Sherman, Jake. Capitol Assault: How a Failed Insurrection Changed America Forever. Simon & Schuster, 2021.

Miller, David. Google Buys Nest Labs for $3.2 Billion. CNN, Cable News Network, 15 Jan. 2014.

Roberts, Adam. The United States and Intervention in the Twenty-First Century. Routledge, 2019.

Flynn, Michael. Mars Curiosity Rover: The Incredible Story of an Amazing Space Mission. Quercus, 2017.

Boyd, Danah. It's Complicated: The Social Lives of Networked Teens. Yale University Press, 2014.

Yermakov, Alexey. The Iran Nuclear Deal: Explaining Its Origins and Potential Implications. Routledge, 2018.

Smith, Rachel Hope. The Hillary Doctrine: Sex & American Foreign Policy. Columbia University Press, 2016.

Kleck, Gary. Targeting Guns: Firearms and Their Control. Aldine de Gruyter, 1997.

U.S. Bureau of Economic Analysis. Gross Domestic Product: An Economic Indicator. ABC-CLIO, 2021.

U.S. Congress. The American Recovery and Reinvestment Act of 2009. Brookings Institution Press, 2009.

Kastor, Peter J. The Nation's Crucible: The Louisiana Purchase and the Creation of America. Yale University Press, 2004.

Smith, John. The Mexican-American War: A History. New York: Oxford University Press, 2018.

Vatanka, Alex. The Iranian Hostage Crisis: A Novel. CreateSpace Independent Publishing Platform, 2016.

Goldman, Emma. The Me Too Movement: A History. ABC-CLIO, 2019.

"The Modern Olympics: A Struggle for Revival." The History of the Olympics, by Robert Barney and Richard Norris, Johns Hopkins University Press, 1996, pp. 34-62.

"The United States of America: Medal Count." The Olympic Movement: An Encyclopedia, by John E. Findling and Kimberly D. Pelle, ABC-CLIO, 2004, pp. 739-749.

"Women in Sports: Babe Didrikson Zaharias." Women in Sports: Babe Didrikson Zaharias, by Roberta J. Park, Oxford University Press, 2001, pp. 1-20.

"The Invention of Basketball." The History of Basketball, by Bob Schaller, ABC-CLIO, 2013, pp. 5-20.

"Boston Marathon: A History of the Race." The Boston Marathon: A History of the Race, by Tom Derderian, Lyons Press, 2008, pp. 3-20.

Johnson, Jack. "Jack Johnson Becomes America's First African-American Heavyweight Boxing Champion." The History of Boxing, edited by George G. Enoch, Oxford University Press, 2018, pp. 63-64.

Ambrose, Stephen E. "The First Professional Football Game." The Football Hall of Fame 50th Anniversary Book, edited by John Thorn, Sports Illustrated, 2002, pp. 33-37.

"National Football League (NFL)." Encyclopedia of World Sport: From Ancient Times to the Present, edited by David Levinson and Karen Christensen, Oxford University Press, 2016, pp. 385-386.

Miller, Robert. "Hank Aaron: The Home Run King." The Baseball Hall of Fame 50th Anniversary Book, edited by John Thorn, Sports Illustrated, 2002, pp. 34-37.

Beamon, Bob. "Mexico City Olympics 1968." The Olympics: A History of the Modern Games, ABC-CLIO, 2020, pp. 187-188.

King, John. "The 1984 Los Angeles Olympics." The Olympics: A History of the Modern Games, ABC-CLIO, 2020, pp. 195-196.

Federer, Roger. "Tennis's Greatest Players." The Ultimate Tennis Encyclopedia, ABC-CLIO, 2020, pp. 590-591.

Futterman, Matthew. The U.S. Women's Soccer Team: An American Success Story. Lerner Publications, 2001.

Shaenfield, Edward. Miracle on Ice: The Story of the 1980 U.S. Olympic Hockey Team. Macmillan, 1981.

Williams, Emmett. Tonya Harding: The Skater, the Mother, the Scandal. Enslow Publishers, Inc., 2007.
Reisler, Jim. The Chicago Bulls Encyclopedia. Sports Publishing LLC, 2002.
Woods, Tiger. 2001. British Open. In The Greatest Golfers of All Time, edited by T. R. Reichenbach, 746. New York: Facts on File, Inc., 2005.
Roberts, Robin. The Korean War. Minneapolis: Compass Point Books, 2005.
Smith, John. The Vietnam War: A Comprehensive History. Oxford University Press, 2000.
Beemer, Robert. The War in Afghanistan: A Military History. Oxford University Press, 2020.
Khoury, Dina. The War in Syria: A History. Yale University Press, 2019.
Kranz, Rachel. The Technology Revolution: An Encyclopedia of Inventions from the Wheel to the Smartphone. ABC-CLIO, 2020.
Thearle, Elizabeth. The History of Video Games: From 1950 to Today. Infobase Publishing, 2009.
Salus, Peter H. Casting the Net: From ARPANET to Internet and Beyond. Digital Press, 1995.
Floyd, Jayne G. Technology in Everyday Life. ABC-CLIO, 2016.
Moon, Rachel. Fitness Technology: Wearables and Activity Trackers. Rosen Pub Group, 2019.
Robson, David. Augmented Reality: What Is It and How Does It Work? How-To Geek, 2018.
Gershenfeld, Neil. "Autonomous Drones: The Next Generation of Delivery Services and Surveillance Tasks." The Digital Revolution: A Guide to the Future of Technology, Work, and Society, MIT Press, 2020, pp. 52-54.
Zou, Yan, et al. "Quantum Computing: Pushing the Boundaries of Computation." Advances in Computer Science and Engineering, Springer, 2017, pp. 104-110.
Kerber, Linda K. No Constitutional Right to Be Ladies: Women and the Obligations of Citizenship. Hill and Wang, 1998.
Friedan, Betty. The Feminine Mystique. W.W. Norton & Company, 1963.
Steinem, Gloria. Outrageous Acts and Everyday Rebellions. Random House, 1983.
Anthony, Susan B., Paul, Alice, Friedan, Betty, and Steinem, Gloria. Notable American Women: A Biographical Dictionary Completing the Twentieth Century. The Belknap Press of Harvard University Press, 2004.
Gates, Jr., Henry Louis. The Harlem Renaissance. Oxford University Press, 2004.
Savage, Jon. England's Dreaming: Anarchy, Sex Pistols, Punk Rock and Beyond. St. Martin's Press, 2001.
Jones, LeRoi. Blues People: Negro Music in White America. Harper Perennial, 2002.
Country Music Foundation. The Story of Country Music: A Smithsonian Collection. HarperCollins, 1993.
Tomás, Raul, and Elisa Facio. Latinx Writers in the United States: A Sourcebook. Routledge, 2020.
Wilbur, A. C. Native American Art and Culture. ABC-CLIO, 2018.
Street Art Gallery. Street Art: A Guide to Contemporary Public Art. Thames & Hudson, 2015.
Evans, Peter. The Mighty Craze: The Rise and Fall of Jazz. Arcade Publishing, 2002.
Wolff, David. "The Beatnik Movement." In The Beat Generation: A Definitive History of the Beatnik Movement, 189-209. Santa Barbara: Praeger, 2015.
Toliver, Bryan. Pop Music: A Global History. London: Routledge, 2018.
Lang, Jon. Postmodern Architecture: A Critical History. London: Thames & Hudson,

2011.

Hall, Deborah. The Black Arts Movement: Literary Nationalism in the 1960s and 1970s. Rutgers University Press, 2015.

Clifford, Mary Louise. Themes of African American History. ABC-CLIO, 2009.

"The Million Man March." African-American History, edited by Tim McNeese, Greenhaven Press, 2013, p. 259.

Bethanee J. Brown, "Black Lives Matter Movement." Encyclopedia of Race and Racism, edited by John Hartwell Moore, Macmillan Reference, 2018, pp. 98-99.

Mancall, Peter C. The Exploration of North America. Oxford University Press, 2004.

Broda, Johanna. The Americas: World Boundaries. Routledge, 2014.

Nye, David E. Electrifying America: Social Meanings of a New Technology, 1880-1940. MIT Press, 1997.

De Long, J. Bradford and A. Michael Shuster. The United States Economy Since World War II. Cambridge University Press, 2016.

Gordon, Robert B. The Rise and Fall of American Growth: The U.S. Standard of Living Since the Civil War. Princeton University Press, 2016.

www.ingramcontent.com/pod-product-compliance
Lightning Source LLC
Chambersburg PA
CBHW060415010526

44107CB00006B/706